Being The Best You!

Jack Walton

Being The Best You!

How to live your best life!

Dedication

Being The Best You has been a personal project of mine that I started in June 2016, since then I've had the pleasure of having some amazing experiences and have met some wonderful people. At times I've left this project for weeks and months in between, leaving it on purpose in order to experience life and its many experiences, which have then given me new insights and have all been shared throughout the book you're about to read.

This book is different, it's a selection of mini chapters, some may be very short, this is because I talk about a large variety of topics which I, Jack Walton, consider important in order for you to live a healthy and happy life. Throughout the book there may be things you both agree and disagree with, which is totally fine. I don't claim to no everything at all, but I know what works for me and I'm now passing it on in the hope it will help you in your life, too.

I'm dedicating this book to my best friend, to the person who bought me into the world, my Mom. I love this human being more than words can say, she's a superhero and truly showed me that if I put my mind to it, absolutely anything is possible. Secondly to my twin sister, who inspires me every day to be my best self and to take every opportunity I'm given, we're both so different but so alike at the same time, I hope this helps you on your very own personal journey too. Finally, to my Nan and Grandpa, my Mom's parents. My Nan died many years ago and I often find myself thinking if she'd be proud of me and how I've turned out and what I've achieved since she left my life at the age of 13. She was the most amazing lady and I think of her often, her class and amazing sense of humor is what I'll cherish most. My Grandpa is someone I've grown so close to in recent years, he's like a Dad I suppose. Thank you for accepting me and my quirks, thank you for always pushing me and supporting me with every experience and opportunity I take on, no matter how crazy it may seem. My friends that are the most amazing support, you all know who you are, thank you! I could go on and on about all the support I've received over the years, I'll never be able to express my gratitude enough, just know it means more than words can describe.

CONTENTS

Chapter 1 – Achieving What You Want: 1

Chapter 2 – Training your Mind: 6

Chapter 3 - Using the Law of Attraction: 14

Chapter 4 – Where Does love Come From? 19

Chapter 5 – The Process: 27

Chapter 6 – How Manifesting Really Works: 33

Chapter 7 – Living in the Moment: 42

Chapter 8 – Our Journey: 49

Chapter 9 - Having a Life Plan: 55

Chapter 10 – The REAL Recipe for Happiness: 62

Chapter 11 - We're all Blessed: 69

Chapter 12 – It's Never too Late to Change: 76

Chapter 13 – Sometimes we have to Let Go: 83

Chapter 14 – Being Equal: 89

Chapter 15 – The "Perfect" Life: 94

Chapter 16 – Putting YOU First: 99

Chapter 17 – Love your Home: 104

Chapter 18 – Putting It into Action: 107

Chapter 19 - Goal Setting is Crucial: 111

Chapter 20 – Wish Upon a Star: 118

Chapter 21 – Are YOU Feeling More Positive Yet? 123

Chapter 22 – My Journey So Far: 127

Chapter 23 – Experiences: 136

Chapter 24 – Are You Stagnating? 144

Chapter 25 – We're ALL Different: 150

Chapter 26 – Inner Beauty: 156

Chapter 27 – We're ALL in This Together: 159

Chapter 28 – Each Day Is a Gift: 166

Chapter 29 – Do Something Different: 169

Chapter 30 – Make the Impossible Possible: 173

Chapter 31 – Life Situations: 179

Chapter 32 – Sometimes we Fall: 185

Chapter 33 – Just do You: 195

Chapter 34 - Rule your Own Mind: 200

Chapter 35 – Focus on what You WANT: 205

Chapter 36 – Take a Break: 209

Chapter 37 – Consistency is Key: 220

Chapter 38 – We're More Similar than we Realise: 225

Chapter 39 – Forgiveness sets us Free: 231

Chapter 40 – Thank You! 241

About the Author: 249

Preface

My names Jack Walton, I'm a 21-year-old student and have a message I want to share, something that has changed my life in ways I never could have imagined, and the best bit, you can do it too.

In just 3 short years I've turned my life around, I went from being an individual with no confidence, low self-esteem and no passion for anything, I was constantly searching for happiness that I just wouldn't find in external things, I wish I had known that at the time. For years I battled with poor mental health, I struggled to fit in and longed to become just half of the person I've become now.

Maybe like you, I was a pretty negative individual, I was suspicious when the positive did happen, questioning and predicting what could happen next to make it all crumble, self-sabotage at its best. I didn't try hard, I didn't work hard towards what I could achieve, after years of struggling with accepting my own sexuality and the knock-on effects of anxiety and PTSD, I didn't like the person I was becoming. If I'm honest and upon reflection, I could see I was on a collision course for disaster, I knew something needed to change.

Within Being The Best You, you will discover what did change and how I found the key to unlock what was always inside of me, myself, my very best self that we all have the power of possessing, you have it right now, even if it doesn't feel like it. I finally realised the key ingredients I needed to be happy, you'd think it's a simple thing, happiness, it really isn't, from being on the journey I find myself on I've finally realised how priceless this is. This is why I'm sharing my message with you now, I can't stay silent now I know what I do, I don't even recognise the Jack that existed just over 3 years ago, I'm living the life I always wanted, of course, I still have challenges, I still have set backs, but the experiences I've had and the person I now am, it's a total transformation.

This book isn't like a usual one, its divided into 40 separate chapters, some are just 1 page long, but I wanted to create a book that speaks about multiple different avenues and subjects, all designed to give you a deeper insight into how you can become a better and happier version of YOU, something I know we all want, no matter who you are. From goal setting, to morning routines, to letting go of the past and living in the social media generation, this book tackles it, along with going deeper into my own personal battles with mental health and accepting my sexuality.

I'm not trained and of course, I don't know everything, but I know what has worked for me and I know it can work for you too. Don't rush this book, it tackles a lot of different areas so feel free to take your time after each chapter to digest its content.

I'm sending you LOVE, LIGHT & ETERNAL HAPPINESS!

Jack xo

Introduction

In today's modern society we now live in it seems that everyone is going at 100 miles an hour. We complain that we don't have enough hours in the day, we are bombarded with social media and the "perfect" looking models who grace our screens, along with this the rise in mental health related issues seen amongst young people is also on the rise, in reality, things are pretty full on and a lot more complicated than they might have been 30 years or so ago. If you're not complaining or feeling depressed everyday about your life and how it's going then what are you doing, that's what it can seem to be most of the time. It's almost like society wants us to be unhappy, it wants us to moan, to complain, from doing this maybe we will be more inclined to spend excess amounts of money on more commercialism in the hopes of it making us feel better, more fulfilled perhaps.

I used to be a sheep, but not anymore. Although I never totally felt like I fitted in amongst the crowd, I did conform to most of the typical norms. I wasn't a happy person, I wasn't happy with where my life was going or what I was achieving, in the hopes of fulfilment I would chase the external constantly, all the while everything I needed existed within... try telling me that a few years back and I would have laughed in your face.

I have a question for you, are you FUFILLED? Are you HAPPY? I'm being serious here, are you actually happy? Because I sure as hell never used to be, not really if I'm being honest. *"That's just too good to be true, things like that don't happy to me"*... just 2 small examples of the statements I used to make, and did they come true... absolutely.

This my friends is a crash course in the Law of Attraction, a term you'll hear referenced a lot more throughout this book. In essence its quite simple, so it baffles me why so many don't know of it, I didn't either until I discovered it through a book on self-love over 3 years ago, when slowly with gradual steps, my life started to change for the better.

I'm not going to bullshit here, nothing changed overnight and anyone who says that is clearly not being honest. The results I have witnessed over the last few years have been down to determination and a lot of SELF BELIEF, having belief in myself and knowing I could achieve more, that I could BE MORE. This isn't overnight but it has been beyond worth it, I've done things I never thought I ever would, I've achieved things that have truly showed me that when you put your mind to something and more importantly, stick at it with absolute conviction, ANYTHING is POSSIBLE.

Within this book you'll discover how YOU can achieve whatever it is you want in your life, you honestly can, its just about getting in the right mindset in order to achieve, in order to win and be the best version of yourself that already exists within, it's just about finding the right key to unlock the door. I have a **4-stage process** that I like to follow, one that works for me and breaks down my dream or goal into smaller chunks.

The first stage is the initial one, to **think it**, before you even have an idea you have to think it up in your mind first right? Second is to **believe it,** instead of having an idea and then straight away being defeatist thinking I can't achieve it (what I used to do!) you really have to start believing it, I mean totally and absolutely believing that you WILL achieve or get whatever it is you're currently wanting. Third is where I put it all into action by **working for it**, when I say working I use that term loosely. For example, a dream of mine was to write a book to help others like I am now, so for the third stage I had to spend years writing it to make it a reality, you can think about it and believe it for as long as you want, but if you don't work for it and start putting plans in place then how do you expect it to happen? If I had believed I was going to write this book but not then lead onto working for it, it wouldn't magically appear in my hands one day, effort is required. The fourth and final step is that from firstly **thinking it,** then **believing it,** then spending time **working for it**, only then, **you will achieve it...** that's the fourth stage, the best one I'm sure you'll agree.

Most people seem to see goals and dreams as a waste, like they can't achieve it so won't bother, but if you have this attitude then how do you ever expect to gain, how do you think things will change if you have such a negative attitude? It can be hard to break a habit of a lifetime, I'm talking from experience here, but I know that no matter what anyone tells me, no matter your age, gender, where you live, financial status or any other factor, YOU can achieve whatever it is you want, YOU can be the person you want to be, you owe it to yourself to live your very BEST LIFE, we only have one, so please, let's not waste it. I'm so happy that you're reading this, and I hope you enjoy discovering the multiple elements within that will all benefit you in some way, no matter how happy or unhappy you might be right now, you can never feel too positive I'm sure you will agree!

Back to the formula! Let's break this down even further, why not grab a pen and some paper and start writing out notes and ideas, anything, just write something down if you're in a space that allows it, if you're travelling why not get up the notes section of your phone and use that instead. Firstly, what do you want? I'm letting you be a kid in a candy store here, what would you like to achieve, what would you like to gain… this could be anything and nothing is too big or too small. Maybe you want to get in a better shape, maybe you want to buy a new car, start a small business, book an abroad holiday, or to just feel more mentally fulfilled, whatever it is, write it down.

Firstly, you need to **think it**, and if you did the last step I asked you to do then this has been achieved.

Secondly, you need to **believe it**, this is something that will take time, it needs to become a reality in your mind, you can't just write it down and then forget about it, if you really want something bad enough you will make sure it's on your mind, you will make sure its within reach, even if it seems like it isn't, just go with it for now. In order to believe it you need to visualise, something you can't do enough of. To visualise means to imagine your goal with it appearing real, make it alive, give it colour, sounds, smells, almost like a movie scene playing out in your mind. In the clip maybe you can see yourself driving a new car down your road, maybe you can see yourself running a 10k marathon and getting over the finish line, whatever it is, you need to start visualising it, DAILY!

Start now, visualise it every morning and every night, like I said, this isn't an instant step and you need to start now! Along with this you need to ensure you can see it daily, you could print out a picture of it and make a vision board, a common practice that I really enjoy doing because it makes it have colour and a physical presence. Stick it where you'll see it, in your bedroom, on your ceiling, on a wall… anywhere that you will pass each day and can spend a few short moments really BELIEVING that soon enough, whatever it is on the photo will become your reality. I don't care how busy you are right now, if you want it badly enough you will make the time to visualise, you will make the time to make the practice a daily priority.

But it doesn't end here, and this is something that I feel is quite conflicting at times amongst those who follow the Law of Attraction, but I want to give my own thoughts. Thinking it and believing it is crucial, having vision boards are something I love because visually its exciting seeing everything you want to achieve in one space. Visualising it in your head I would say is even more crucial, because the mind can't determine what is real and what is in your head, that's why if you feel fear about something that might not be happening right now, you'll still feel fear like its taking place, you'll feel anxious. The same applies with visualising, your mind doesn't know that the vision isn't real yet, its powerful and does work... I know there will be sceptics amongst you, which is funny, because I used to be the exact same, until I learnt what I know now.

Some people say that after the 2 steps I've just given its fast forward to achieving it, in my personal opinion I don't believe that to be the case. That's why I have the third step which is to **work for it,** if you don't do something physical, how do you expect it to appear? This step is crucial because it's you putting into place actual steps to achieve. If you want a new car maybe you ask for more shifts at work, perhaps you create a spreadsheet and start spending time budgeting to put aside extra money. If you want a healthy body along with visualising the end result you then spend time putting in the work at the gym, eating the right foods, creating a good routine etc. See how important the third step is? Even if you're reading this not knowing of what physical steps to take, they are there, trust me, you just need to spend some time thinking of what you can do extra to achieve it. I like to think of this exercise as a steppingstone to achieve the end result.

Each stage is a steppingstone, which directly leads onto the next. However, you don't just do the one at a time and then stop doing it, it's a process of DOING ALL 3 at the same time which then leads to you achieving it. Again, it could be argued that it doesn't sound easy but whenever I have a goal or dream I challenge it, because if I want it bad enough and have that much passion for it I know I'd walk over hot coals, so doing this process is absolutely possible. So, before moving on with reading why not spend a good 20 minutes having a think of what it is you want, what do you want to achieve? Not your family, not your friends but YOU, because this is what the book is about, becoming your best self, because I know for sure the majority aren't being that, so let's change it!

Chapter 1
Achieving What You Want

You CAN achieve whatever you want in your life. Start by completely erasing the word can't from your vocabulary. It's such a limiting word. As soon as you say a sentence out loud with the word can't it will immediately make your brain feel more limited and obviously you will be more likely to believe it. When you're trying your absolute hardest in whatever it is you're doing you will get stressed and feel like the finishing line is nowhere near in sight. Anything negative in my opinion does not have the right to live or be there in your mind or body, you should be allowed to think and feel as many positive thoughts as you want.

Go to the mirror, look at yourself in the eye and say, *"I CAN do it"*, say this at least 20 times. From my own experience, I find saying things out loud completely destroys the negative thoughts and I immediately start feeling better and more positive, different things work for different people, it's all about finding what works best for you. Another thing you need to start doing if you are constantly feeling negative and stressed out is some form of relaxation, this one isn't always the most well received but it's to meditate, something I've been practicing now for 3 years. I can definitely say that the first time you meditate you will feel so weird and you will feel like it won't help. Concentrate firstly on your breathing, deeply breath and feel every muscle in your body relax into a lovely warm state of comfort. Think happy thoughts throughout this if you wish or just let the words wash over your mind and body as your mind relaxes, probably for the first time in ages.

The reason many of us don't like the idea of meditation is because we have to stop and have time to think, sometimes in our busy lives we don't want to have time to stop and think, especially if what we're thinking isn't particularly good. With meditation many think they are doing it wrong if they have lots of thoughts come up, that's totally NORMAL, when I meditate, I'll still have thoughts pop up occasionally about what I want for dinner or something else like that, so don't beat yourself up if it takes a while to get used to it. It's so much easier to relax your body, think of it like taking a hot bath, but for your mind instead. Most people are so focused on going to the gym and making their bodies the best they can be, instead meditating for around 20 minutes a day is just the same as visiting a mind gym of sorts. You can still go to the gym and live your day to day life but 20 minutes of meditation either in the morning or evening will be so beneficial in the long-term.

You won't find instant results but with all the things I recommend after as little as 4 weeks you will start feeling differently, it's not overnight change but when you combine multiple techniques like this it does make a lasting difference. When I first started these techniques I noticed that things didn't really change physically but the way I looked at things and the way I mentally thought completely changed. People talk about the power hour where you complete 20 minutes of exercise, 20 minutes of meditation and 20 minutes of reading. Putting some time into you will be extremely beneficial to your life and you will actually feel like things aren't as complicated or stressful as you first thought. Over time you will feel like most of the time you were zooming in on the tiny problems and issues which felt like major problems, when actually this is not the case and really in the grand scheme of things they're pretty small and won't stop you living a life that YOU so true fully deserve, you always have deserved happiness.

No matter what shit life throws at you, you can be happy. It's like when we speak to a friend or family member about a problem we might be experiencing, and they don't seem to see what all the fuss is about, it's because that when an outside influence is looking from the outside it isn't always as bad as what we make it out to be in our heads, it can seem so much worse than what it actually is, because a lot of the time we catastrophize, don't we, we come up with all the bad things that could happen, where ultimately its OURSELVES making us feel like this, no one else.

<u>Reactions</u>

The way you react to certain situations can mean you feel more unhappy too, sometimes without realising it. Let's say you and your colleagues at work are all desperately trying to get a promotion which has been offered up by your boss. Your best friend and colleague is successful with getting the promotion. Yes, you didn't get the promotion but it's not the end for you, even though at the time it may seem like it. You react by completely blanking your friend after this and create an atmosphere within the office. Who decided to react like this, no one but you! By doing this you now feel even worse and get into a slump of complete depression and anger over your friend getting the promotion, but really, you're not angry at your friend your angry at yourself as you feel unworthy of success which is complete bullshit!

Instead it could have completely gone differently. You hear your friend got the promotion and instead you congratulate them, and all go out for a drink after. Instead you will feel a lot better a hell of a lot quicker instead of becoming even more negative with doing option 1. Sometimes the way we react to certain situations can have a huge impact on our own life, even though we don't see this because some people have been thinking negatively about themselves like this for years and don't know any different, well you do now, you are special, you are worthy and deserve wealth and abundance within your life no matter what anyone else tells you for that matter, you know the truth. I bet after me giving you this example scenario you can straight away think of your own of where you've made things a lot harder on yourself by reacting a certain way in a situation, it's so easy to blow up and let the jealousy or hurt consume, but actually, it's funny really because it's just as easy to walk away and say, no, I'm not going to get angry, petty or jealous, I'm not going to go low, instead, I'm going to walk on by and leave this alone, because I'm BETTER THAN THIS and I deserve more than this.

It's almost like we have the angel on one shoulder and the devil on the other. Sure, you probably think at the time that it's fun and is making you feel better to listen to the devil and be consumed by it, but after the situation dies down and you start to gain more clarity of the situation, is it really making you feel better… probably not.

Chapter 2
Training your Mind

I came up with the title of Being The Best You because that's what I want, most of us are nowhere near being the best versions of ourselves, most of us are just an average version and could be so much happier by just changing the way we think and view things. Physical things are good but starting with the mental challenges can sometimes be harder. I found that training my mind to start thinking positive thoughts about myself and life actually felt abnormal but eventually I things started to change and now I try to laugh at my mistakes instead of going mad and getting in a mood, something I used to do quite frequently. When you get to that level and you're vibrating on a higher frequency you'll feel so amazing, yes, challenges and situations will present themselves because this is life and it's perfect for NO ONE, but with a healthy mindset I do feel the way we handle things is so much better and healthier for us.

Remember, we're only human, it's impossible to be positive and happy every single day for the rest of our lives, this won't happen and of course sometimes I will have a down day or a down moment, sometimes I have down days and have to take the time to work out why I'm feeling the way I'm feeling, because usually for me, there will always be an underline reason as to why I'm feeling like it, it's about being your own best friend and not beating yourself up for having bad moments, because it's absolutely OK to feel like shit, it's OK to feel like you don't want to adult today and do the things you know you should be doing, it's OK to take a minute and just BE, sometimes we feel like we need to be going 24/7 and always doing something just to keep up with it all, but in reality we don't. It can feel like the entire planet is going at 100 miles an hour, but then when you go somewhere secluded or out in the country you realise how SLOW the world really is, the sea isn't rushing, the animals aren't rushing, its US making us feel like we need to be, so, take some time when you need to, you'd think this would be common sense, but at the same time it's harder to realise in a world that seems to be busier and busier.

When you have a down moment the key thing is to not let it consume you and completely take over your day and ruin everything you were planning on doing. This is something I used to do so much. Having a down moment and then almost subconsciously wanting it to make you feel worse and moodier, maybe this is because that on a deeper level we feel negatively about ourselves and don't really care if bad things or experiences happen to us, maybe because we get to a point where we don't expect any less, we expect bad things to happen, probably because we're so used to thinking negatively. This all goes back to how thinking like this can have a serious impact on your life and overall health, mentally and physically. Do you ever notice how when you feel negative and feel down, that your physical health gets worse? You feel more tired, practically exhausted and overworked all the time. This isn't because we are physically poorly, it may seem like it, but that's not the case.

Sometimes just thinking negatively and being in a bad head space can make us feel worse physically and can actually make us believe there is something physically wrong when really there isn't anything wrong at all. This made me realise how powerful the mind is, the power of the mind is so strong that it can determine our whole entire lives, just by the way we think. This sounds completely bizarre but it's so true, and the time you have that light bulb moment like I did once, is the time your life will start to drastically improve for the better, little by little. My aim is that through this book, you'll learn more about yourself and what you truly want to do with your life, this is time for YOU, no one else.

This takes us back to the Law of Attraction, when you think positive, positive things will happen and the same for when you think negatively about yourself and others, negative things will happen. Studies have shown that when people think positive thoughts about themselves and the world around them, that overall, they will live a happier life, just by slightly adjusting the way you think, it's so simple when you actually think about it. The thing is many of us aren't used to thinking positive about ourselves, we feel silly and when I first started thinking more positive about myself and the world around me, I have to admit the only world I can use to describe it is that it felt strange. As I carried on it felt more and more normal, now I could never imagine not thinking positive thoughts about myself, as I continued I felt so much happier, even when things weren't going right that was alright because I was in a completely different head space and didn't get as phased by things, the levels of stress I used to feel over the tiniest of things, like with my appearance or if the slightest thing went wrong, it would feel like the end of the world.

I think its ridiculously easy to be the same as everyone else, because when you think about it, a lot of society are the same, they think and act the same, they have a negative outlook on life, they complain, moan and wonder why things aren't improving for the better. It's easy to agree with your friends and family and join the choir of complainers, I'm talking from years of experience. If you have someone in your own life who isn't like this, maybe start spending some time in their company, they might have more of a happy take on things than the average, I bet they get more joy and fulfilment out of life too. Looking at our relationships is something I go into a lot more detail later on.

Chapter 3

Using the Law of Attraction

Let's go over the official definition of the Law of Attraction, because you may not know that this is not something made up, it's in fact an actual law dating back thousands of years and has been used so much by so many people and has completely changed their lives for the better. *"The law of attraction is the name given to the maxim like attracts like"* which in New Thought philosophy is used to sum up the idea that by focusing on positive or negative thoughts a person brings positive or negative experiences into their life. This could not be simpler, the universe will forever be listening to your thoughts and what you say, be that out loud or in your head, the universe always listens and manifests what you ask for, be that good or bad. The universe does not know the difference between good or bad things, if you go looking for bad things or experiences it won't be too long before you find them, the complete same rule applies for positive things and experiences, the universe will forever be listening.

If you don't physically think you're looking for negative experiences, you might keep subconsciously thinking negative which means the universe hears this and then manifests it to you in the form of something good or bad. If used correctly by visualizing what you want every day, showing gratitude for the things and people you do have in your life and you are grateful for will honestly transform your life and may even make you realise that your current situation isn't as bad as you had first thought, your negative thinking was actually making things worse but because you got so deep in your negative situation you couldn't actually determine you were doing this.

An example, can you think of a time where although you may not have said it out loud, ended up experiencing something that you were previously thinking about in your head, maybe you think you predicted something bad that happened, you might have spent so long cooking up the pretend situation that it eventually ended up becoming your reality... I'm sure we can all come up with one. You, without realising it, were using the Law Of Attraction, but in the wrong way, you thought about the negative situation long enough it ended up happening... the exact same can happen for a positive one but I know what we're all thinking, it's so much easier to think of the negative first before the positive, WHY IS THIS?! I don't have a solid answer other than conditioning; generations have spent so many years in the same mindset of negative thinking that it seems odd and weird to change a habit of a lifetime, but you've just got to trust me, it will be more than worth your while in the long run.

So, tips for finding out more about the Law of Attraction. Firstly, I strongly recommend that you go and do some simple research into it, there are some amazing resources and books out there, the most famous called "The Secret" by Rhonda Byrne. It's a bestselling self-help book and honestly, it's the best thing I ever discovered in terms of the Law of Attraction and positive thinking, it breaks it down and makes it much easier to understand without any scientific jargon. Just like I said earlier this book claims that positive thinking can create life-changing results such as increased happiness, better health, wealth and abundance. It's also been made into a film; I highly recommend that you check it out.

Another recommendation I have regarding the Law of Attraction is watching YouTube videos on it, there are so many simple ones that break it down and make it much easier to understand, spend some time listening to videos that give stories of how multiple people around the world have utilized it and achieved things that on the surface didn't always seem possible, YouTube is full of thousands of them, so if you're interested and, why wouldn't you be, definitely give a few a watch for yourself when you get some spare time.

Chapter 4

Where Does love Come From?

I'm no expert, but I do know that the power of positivity and the power of self-development could make a huge improvement in your life from what I've personally experienced in just 3 short years. I'm saying this because I want to tell anyone who is reading, no matter what your situation, that things probably do seem bad and that there is no way out, but things will gradually start to change and improve if you do these things I have so far spoken about. I'm not rich living in a mansion with a Ferrari saying this, I'm just someone who changed their life through their mind, now I know what I know I can't keep all this to myself, I have to tell others, all I want to do is help people and inspire you to be your very best self, I want to show you that no matter where you live, no matter how much money you have or don't have, ANYTHING is possible with a little belief and hard work, I strongly believe that anyone can be their best self. Life isn't all about material things, there's so much more to life and so much more happiness and abundance which can come from inside yourself, it doesn't cost a penny.

Ever heard of a millionaire who has everything and was forever stressed and constantly thinking about the next thing, never actually enjoying their life and the things they worked so hard to manifest? This can happen because while all this was going on, they completely forgot to take care of their own wellbeing, and even though they have all these material things they're not actually HAPPY with themselves. There is so much more to life than the latest car or trend. Obviously, I can't lie, these things are nice and might seem enjoyable, but I then realised that, although I did enjoy material things, they didn't really make me happy, even when I wanted them to. They didn't make me happy and didn't really contribute anything to my life, apart from making me even greedier and not enjoying the things I already had, I completely forgot about those things and was constantly obsessed with the next.

This is just my experience though, yours could be completely different which is fine because we're all different and all have a different perspective on life and what makes us happy. If you're someone who is very successful and are at a place mentally where you're happy with yourself and want to have material things, then have them. I love shopping, when I say love, I mean bloody LOVE, I love buying clothes and expressing myself. My past experience with this wasn't a good one, for me I'd buy clothes to make me happy, because I wasn't happy at all, I thought that buying them and spending money would fill a void I was desperately trying to fill, and when I'd get the clothes home and put them away that same old empty feeling would return, only for me to do the same thing again in order to carry on trying to feel better within myself, where all the while everything I needed wasn't waiting at the shopping mall, it was within ME, and it cost £0. When you get to a point in realising that everything we as humans need is within us, it's pretty life changing. Of course it's great to wear nice clothes and get your hair done, we all do this, and I love making an effort with my appearance, but I also realise that everything I really need is internally, not externally, sit with that one for a while and just consider it.

Challenges we Face

In life you will always face challenges, some good and some not so good, but this is part of life. It's all about taking the good with the bad and not beating yourself up when you do mess up. Let's say the challenge you're facing is whether to stay in a dead-end job or quit and setup your own business. There will be many obstacles to come if you go down this route of setting up your own business, but at the same time you'll be doing something you love, and it will be so worth it. When facing difficult challenges, I find that taking a risk and jumping in headfirst is the bravest thing to do. From my own experiences I know at times we see a challenge coming up or something we want to do in our lives, and we sit and think about all the bad and negative things that might happen if we do it. Such as the business example, you might think things like going bankrupt or your business failing in some way. Again, many people think negative things like this, and it really gets us nowhere, it just makes us more reluctant to actually give it a go and do the things that make us the happiest, usually because they scare us the most.

So, when we have these thoughts of exciting things we want to do or something we want to achieve, because of all the mind rubbish I spoke about earlier, this clouds our judgment and dirties the water, meaning that 9 times out of 10 we end up ditching the idea and not acting on it... does this sound familiar? Because if we're honest, it's so much easier to carry on as we always have, it's easier to do the safe option, because that's what we've been taught, it's the logical thing to do right? It's almost like that head vs heart game of tennis that goes back and forth.

Your head is useful because usually it's the logistical side, it tells us the facts and informative details which are usually pretty boring and dull, but nevertheless are needed from time to time. When choosing what you really want to do yes you need to be practical, yes be realistic about how you're going to do it and if it's the right thing for you, but also remember to listen to your heart too. Listening to your heart tells you what you truly want and also how you really feel. A mixture of both is best but don't let the negative thoughts and even opinions or influences of people close to you affect what you want to do with YOUR life. Always remember when deciding to do something who is in control and who is in charge of their own destiny, little old YOU is the answer! It's so easy to take on the opinions of others, particularly those closest to us who we have an emotional connection to, it's easy to doubt ourselves when we're doubted by those we love. They aren't living your life though are they, their living their OWN LIFE and you're living yours, so it's about kindly taking on board any opinions you're given, and then throwing them out… joking! In reality its considering the opinions but then having time alone to think what you really want, what will make you happy, not your friends, family or boyfriend, but you!

The debate of head vs heart is certainly a hard one, when you ask others what they usually listen to when making decisions I imagine you'd get a variety of different answers. For me I usually go with my heart, but then listen to what my head is saying because usually my head will go for the sensible option, I guess that's the part of myself that is scared of taking risks and giving things a go and seeing what happens. I've certainly had experiences where I've listened to my heart and it hasn't ended up going to plan, that's ok too though, because at least I tried and gave something a go, which is much better than just sitting there with a thought and not having the courage to act on it, easier said than done I know. What I've realised more and more is that life is so short when you think about it, so why are people so precious about it and what they do? For me now if I want to do something different that yes, may not workout, I'll still give it a try because I'd rather say I gave it a try and it didn't work well instead of saying I didn't try at all. Please don't end up saying you could have had lots of experiences and doing lots of different things but chose not to due to you being afraid, or a negative influence off someone else, because once its game over that's it. People are too precious when it comes to taking risks, of course as I've said, they won't always pay off, but if you don't at least try, you'll never know, so, for your own sake and happiness, let's give it a go.

Chapter 5

The Process

You honestly can do and be anything you want to be if you seriously put your mind to it and do the 4-step process I always try and live by. To recap its: **THINK IT**, **BELIEVE IT**, **WORK FOR IT**, then you will **ACHIEVE IT!** It's really as simple as that. Think about what you want every day, then think positive thoughts through visualization and mediation by believing you can achieve and do it, then put the practical steps into place by working for what you want, this step will be the longest and most time consuming but so worth it, then you will achieve it, the fourth and final step. This four-stage process can be used for whatever you want to manifest within your life, no matter how big or small! Let's say you're a student who wants to buy their first car. Let's go through the process together.

First you **THINK IT**, you decide you want to purchase your first car, then you **BELIEVE IT**, you visualize that car EVERY SINGLE DAY, you visualize yourself sitting in it, driving it, going to fun places in it. Do whatever it takes to start believing it, print out a photo and stick it on your wall or ceiling so you see it every morning. Next is **WORK FOR IT,** ok so you decide to apply for a part time job whilst studying, you decide to take up extra shifts… I'm being honest now and ZERO BULLSHIT, yes, it might take a while, but you can ABSOLUTELY DO IT, if you want it bad enough, you'll find ways to achieve it, no matter what it may be. Finally, it might be a year later, it might be a few months, but after thinking it, believing it, visualizing it within this, working for it, you'll then **GET IT!** Of course, it isn't always simple as just that, but I absolutely promise you, using this process will make what you want to happen a hell of a lot quicker.

By visualizing just once daily, maybe on your morning commute, its bringing to life what you want to achieve, it's like a perfect Hollywood film and you're bringing to life your goals. It might seem weird but even start telling people about your goals too before they happen, this is something I do because at the same time it's also holding me accountable, its making me think that because I'm telling people about it, I better make it happen so I can show people the results. No goal is too small and in reality, non is too big either, it's all down to how much effort you want to put in and how much you want it to happen, like with most things, dedication and consistency is key.

Consideration

One of the sayings in life I live by is to treat others as you wish to be treated. I heard this first in school by my head teacher and have applied it to my life ever since. When you're in a situation and someone does something against you, maybe you've had a disagreement or argument with someone for example. You can't just be so quick to judge someone until you've been in their shoes and walked their journey. I learnt not so long ago that as humans and busy people we're so wrapped up within our own lives, we also need to consider and think about how that person feels and what experiences and hardships they've had in their life to make them like this. This is just another tip to apply and think about in your everyday life. This is why I wrote this book, I have so many thoughts and feelings that are so simple and easy to apply to your own lives. The thing is we all have the skills and tools in our minds to do this, but most of us don't use the tools in order to achieve the happiness we want. NOBODY can honestly say they don't know how to be happy. Yes, it is possible that you've been in such a negative headspace for such a long time that the case is that you've forgotten how to be happy because all you can think is negative thoughts about yourself and the world around you. You have the skills and tools right now in order to be happy it's just that maybe the tools are slightly rusty and haven't been used for such a long time. Go into your headspace and seek out the tools you need in order to change your life and to restore the happiness YOU so clearly deserve!

Ok, lets focus on the **4-stage process**, and look at stager 3, work for it, in order to work for anything we need some steppingstone in place, small steps, lets label them goals, to make whatever you want a reality.

Let's say your biggest dream is to become a doctor. Firstly, you do everything you possibly can to achieve your dream. You study hard at medical school; you visit hospitals for work placements etc. When you get negative feedback from others around you based on what you're doing or want to do, you have to be sure to NOT let that get to you or bother you, which isn't always so easy because as humans we really care about what other people think of us and what we're doing, because ultimately we're seeking approval when we don't always have it for ourselves. I've heard of countless examples of people saying they have decided to give up on their dream because their family or friends think it's stupid or say it's too hard for them. The actual truth is that NOTHING is too hard for you to achieve, nothing is too hard for you to do or obtain within your life, no matter what it is. It all boils down to how much EFFORT you want to put in, in order to achieve what you want. If you believe you can do it then you will do it, if you believe and tell yourself you can't then you won't, it really is as simple as that! This again is where the Law of Attraction comes into the picture.

Chapter 6

How Manifesting Really Works

No matter what thoughts you think in your mind, be that good ones or bad, they all resonate with the universe. You ultimately manifest exactly what you want and what you're thinking. For example, you say and think to yourself that today is going to be a terrible day at work, that your boss is going to shout at you and things generally are going to be bad. The honest answer is that something negative most likely will happen. Unfortunately, if the majority of people knew this in the first place they probably wouldn't be negative and think badly about themselves to begin with. I know this isn't possible all of the time, but if we all realised just how powerful our own thoughts are, we'd think and choose them much more carefully, it's easy to think that it's just the words we speak out loud that have an impact, but the internal thoughts are just as important, you might try and speak positively but still have a world of negativity internally and wonder why things aren't working out the way you want them to, this is why.

That's why I'm sharing this with you, I spent so long thinking negatively about certain situations and kept wondering why they weren't getting better and what I was doing wrong. The truth is the thing I was doing wrong was constantly thinking negatively about the situation, thinking negatively like this is clearly a method of destruction and will never work, anyway, thinking those kind of thoughts is just wasted headspace and doesn't deserve to live within your mind or body... we're all beautiful humans, shouldn't we be more considered with how we fill our own minds?! Sadly, we're all too used to thinking negatively about ourselves, for some unknown reason, a lot of people find it easier to point out the negatives and think badly about themselves instead of being positive and paying themselves a compliment for doing well. In England especially, when we're given a compliment am I the only one who immediately brushes it off, like if someone likes your outfit and you say you've had it ages or another similar statement.... It's so weird and certainly something I've noticed that I do at times! For you to succeed and move further within your life and within yourself this really needs to change.

Having a negative attitude and living within a negative headspace means that any success is highly unlikely. Like I said, negative thoughts are just wasted headspace for all the lovely positive thoughts you SHOULD be thinking in order to manifest and obtain whatever it is you need or want. You can never be too greedy when it comes to asking for the things you want within your life, ask for them because the Universe will hear every single thing you ask for, good or bad. But, before we ask for everything we want, one of the best things we can do first is to show appreciation and gratitude for everything we ALREADY have, most of the time we take the most important things for granted.

Gratitude

Believe it or not, one of the simplest things in life can actually be one of the most powerful if used correctly! One of the saddest things is that most of us naturally take things for granted within our lives without realising until it's too late. Such as when the item or pleasure is taken away from us, only then do we realise how much we actually enjoyed it, like when something goes wrong with our health only then we realise how much freedom we had to enjoy and live our lives without any health worries. Taking things for granted really has been proven to be one of the worst things you could do. I can hold my hands up and say this is certainly something I have done in my life and it ultimately gives a negative outcome in most situations and makes you feel worse in the long run. Most people do this without even knowing, most likely because they've been doing it for such a long time. Try to show gratitude in your day to day life as much as you possibly can, it will seem strange at first. For example, say things like "I'm so grateful for my job" or "I'm so grateful to be alive and healthy", the most basic one which many of us forget to say or think about in our busy lives.

All of these are perfect examples of ways you can show gratitude in order to make your life even better than it is already. Once you start writing down or thinking about your blessings you will feel so much more positive about your current situation and will soon realise there is so many good aspects to your life than you first realised. Even when things aren't going your way or you're having some kind of negative experience, whatever it is there is always something to be grateful for in EVERY single situation. Like I said even if things couldn't get any worse for you or you feel like that anyway, you can always be grateful for just being ALIVE and show gratitude this way. The universe does and always will listen when you show gratitude. You can show gratitude for so many things like your job, health, financial status, food & water, love, happiness, material objects, public services, your home and family etc. These are all things you can show gratitude to the universe for.

I like to get some paper and write down what I'm grateful for, practically all the tips I recommend throughout this book cost £0, but they make you feel pretty damn awesome in the process. Give it a go, what are you grateful for? Let's start with the most basics, if you're reading this book then you have sight, right? Can you walk, can you use your hands, can you smell, can you hear… these are all major things to be grateful for and blessings that so many people don't have. Do you have a roof over your head, do you have food and water, do you have clothes to wear, do you own a car, do you live in a country free from war…? I could go on and on. So, if at the beginning of me talking about showing gratitude you were thinking to yourself that you don't have much to be grateful for… how about now?! What I do each day is go over my gratitude list, it could be on paper, I have mine within the notes section of my phone, for me looking at it each morning is the most effective, because it gets you in a proactive and happy mindset before the day begins.

Before you carry on reading I want you to get out your phone, or just a piece of paper, and write down a list of everything you're grateful for, starting with the basics I just spoke about, then the bigger things such as materials, then people, experiences etc. I reckon you'll get at least 10 on there in no time at all, let's go!

Counting your Blessings

Just simply counting your blessing every morning could have such a positive effect on your life. For example, if you are currently finding yourself in a negative financial situation where you have little or no money, make sure to show gratitude for the little money you do have. This way the universe hears that you are grateful for the money you do have instead of moaning and complaining about it all the time, this way more money will then manifest itself in your life through simply saying this out loud or in your head… eventually! Whenever you practice gratitude don't forget to say the simplest thing, which is "thank you". We were all taught this as a child, but many don't realise how powerful this actually is, just saying this the universe will immediately hear and will be so happy you're counting the blessings you do have instead of constantly wanting more, think about the things you do have for a change, I can promise you you'll instantly feel better by doing this and will realise how much you have and how much you have to be grateful for. Write a list, make a collage on your wall, anything where you can articulate and remember how much you have, especially in the hard times when you need it the most. Personally from looking at my list at the start of each day it immediately puts me in a good mood and healthier mindset. On mornings when I wake up and sometimes don't really feel it, I make sure to start going over my gratitude list and the way it lifts my mood instantly is pretty epic, and again, everyone has a few minutes to spare if they really want to. Besides, we make the time to scroll through our social media, so we absolutely have the time for this!

Chapter 7

Living in the Moment

In our daily lives, most of us never stop and think about the moment we're currently in and the feelings we're currently experiencing. We lead incredibly busy lives and most of us are constantly thinking about the future and the next big thing we want to buy or the next thing we want to do, this can be a good thing, but it also means we forget about the present and are forever obsessing over the future or sometimes the past. Past experiences can't be changed, many people really need to realise this. So many people spend their time thinking about something they previously did or said or what they didn't. There is ZERO POINT in thinking about the past and having regrets about something we did or something someone else did, don't EVER let regret consume you. Regret really is one of the worst emotions, it really doesn't have the right to live in our bodies and only causes us further pain and suffering… because we can't change it and desperately want too, that's what the issue is.

We all think about the past but what many people don't consider is that you can't change it, the past is the past but the amazing wonderful thing, is that everyone has the power to change their FUTURE! You can change your future and make it whatever you want it to be. Many people spend so much time complaining and being depressed over their current situation, relationship, or job, why do you do this, do you honestly think it will change anything or make you feel any better… of course it won't, which is common sense when you properly think about it. In order to live a happy and healthy life you need to stop obsessing over the past and work on your present situation in the state it is in right now at this very moment, then your future will take care of itself and will turn out exactly as you want it to.

Constantly thinking about the past has also been proven to make you more depressed and live in a negative mindset in the future, so just let go and bless the past no matter what happened, of course I know this isn't always easy, but you can write your future without getting rid of any of the previous chapters of your life. Our previous chapters are written now and nothing else can be done but it doesn't mean the whole book has to be bad and definitely won't be if you take control in order to get the future that YOU want. I used to spend so much time thinking about the past and future that I never enjoyed the beautiful experiences that were happening at the time in the present, instead I was wishing the days away till the weekend when I was doing something exciting, I was totally disregarding all the great experiences that could have been happening within the meantime, I was like a magnet repelling them and I do realise and understand from looking back that I was ultimately blocking a lot of good things from happening in my life, including meeting amazing people and going to great places, I was just wishing the days away... does this sound familiar at all? It's almost like with Mondays, why are we constantly made to hate it, it's just a day, like Saturday, but people seem to love Saturday, so why not Monday?

I used to dread Mondays, I suppose because I felt like I had to because that's what the crowd did, ultimately, I was a sheep without realising it. But then as I progressed within my mindfulness and positive thinking I started questioning all my old beliefs and thought patterns and realised how damaging they were to my mental health, I stopped hating Mondays and started loving them, because if I don't enjoy them I have to take charge of myself and ask why, it's not my parents fault, it's not my friends fault, its mine, because I'm responsible for my own happiness, and so are you. So, if you're reading this and also don't like Mondays, stop reading and sit with the thought for a little bit, prod and poke it before getting to the source, because there is surely a bigger reason as to why, isn't there? Do or change something so you enjoy them more, maybe realistically you can't leave the job you hate, well physically you can but maybe to you it seems the risks would be too big and you wouldn't be able to cope... fine, so what small steps can you implement to ensure your week starts on a better note?

Relating to the Monday example and Another mantra I live by in my life is the saying "nothing is forever", always remember that whatever situation you are in, especially if it's a negative upsetting one, is that nothing is forever, things and circumstances will change just because they have to, things must change at certain points and therefore your situation WILL GET BETTER. Just remember to show gratitude to the universe for your current experience, even if it is bad there will always be something to be grateful for no matter what sort of situation you find yourself in, again, just being alive is the simplest. By showing gratitude, it shows the universe that you do appreciate the little things and are grateful for the small blessings in life, like food and drink for example, it's one of the key things in life in order for us to survive and thrive, but many forget this. Just showing gratitude before you eat or drink something is showing you understand on a deeper and more concentrated level that you're grateful for every blessing that comes into your life, even the small ones that we forget in our busy lives. Showing gratitude for your life is much better than sitting around complaining about it.

I honestly struggle at times and try to get my head around why it is people think that moaning and complaining about how bad things are, actually think this will make things change and get better for them, guess what? IT WONT. Complaining and moaning gets us nowhere and after you have complained about how bad things are in your life you may feel better and think you were getting it off your chest, actually it's the complete opposite and will make you feel worse. This also means that you're showing the universe that you're not grateful for the small blessings in your life and are therefore not going to have a better future and the little gratitude you do have for aspects of your life will eventually be taken away from you, it's basically a downward spiral, which is why I say again that you must always be grateful for everything you receive, no matter how insignificant!

Chapter 8

Our Journey

Another thing I've implemented over the last few years is choosing to not look back at my past in a negative way. This is one of the worst things you could choose to do, it will most likely make you feel worse, especially if you feel like you've made bad decisions and choices... and I repeat myself again, we can't get that time back. I realised that as soon as I stopped looking back and analyzing everything that I instantly felt better, I now only look back to reflect, like reflecting on my progress from the previous month, so yes, looking back can be beneficial in that way, this is constructive looking back, the opposite to what I used to do. Looking back in a positive way to see how your life has improved and changed for the better is such a powerful thing to do and really gives you an immense feeling of pride and upliftment, just try it for yourself... what are you proud of, no matter how small, I know for sure you've achieved something. Even if you're looking back thinking that you did well but could have done better, immediately stop thinking like that, because at least you tried in the first place, people are way too hard on themselves for too much of the time.

This also brings me on to being too self-critical of yourself and taking every single thing far too seriously, again something I've majorly been guilty of in the past. When you make mistakes, even small ones, don't be too hard on yourself and get stressed out. It's not the end of the world and guess what? We mess up because we're HUMAN. When you make any mistake in the future you need to learn to laugh at yourself and just get on with the rest of your day. Don't cry, don't shout, and don't constantly work yourself up or beat yourself up, it really won't get you anywhere in the long run, trust me. I know this is easier said than done but you really will benefit in the long run if you learn to accept your mistakes. Of course, learn from your mistakes in the meantime and then get on with your day or whatever it is you were doing prior to this. That way you will deflect the situation much quicker and will be less likely to get upset and remove it from your headspace. Always remember that NO ONE is able to thrive in a negative headspace, no one can do things with ease in a negative headspace, it's just not possible, because everything feels ten times harder than what it is, even the small tasks, everything takes up so much of your energy and feels like a mountain to climb, that's how awful negative self-talk can be.

In order to do things quickly and efficiently you need to live in a positive headspace whenever you can. Obviously, I can definitely say no matter what anyone says it's impossible to be positive all of the time, we all have down moments and we wouldn't be human if we were happy and positive 24/7, actually showing emotion and sometimes having a good cry and chance to reflect actually helps in moving forward, you're not a robot so don't feel bad about showing emotions. I used to think that showing emotion and crying was a sign of weakness, as a boy especially if I ended up crying over anything, I'd label myself as pathetic and silly, I'd ridicule myself for getting to that level. However, showing emotion and crying especially is so good for us, letting it all out and then moving forward after is much better than bottling it all up I'm sure you'd agree. Now I know this I'm so open with my emotions, I always joke that things that are sad make me cry and then things that are happy make me cry too, I'm a much more emotionally open person now than what I once was throughout my teenage years growing up. If you're a man reading this, I'm sure you can relate too, in society we're taught that it's a weakness to cry and show emotion, that somehow, it makes us less of a man… what a load of bollocks is that? It's no wonder so many men take their own lives because they felt like they couldn't speak out and be themselves, something that little by little is starting to change, so if you're reading this and relating, have a little cry, and be kind to yourself in the process.

Self-Analysing

This brings me on to analysing, of course it can be a good thing, but if done obsessively it can be a bad thing for your mind and body. When things happen to you in your life be that good or bad, we tend to think they are too good to be true, especially the good things… why is it we do that, it's almost like we get suspicious when things are going well, this is certainly how I used to think! When something good happens to you it's no coincidence. When good things happen to you it's happening because you have shown an immense amount of gratitude in your life and this is the universe rewarding you by giving you what you want, be that your dream car, house or even career. I found that over analysing certain things within your life can really bring more negativity into your life because subconsciously it means you're doubting if you deserve what is happening, especially if it's a good thing. I learnt quickly that in order to find peace and be happy within yourself you need to completely stop over analysing things. For example, I know for sure I've been in situations in the past where really good things have happened, maybe a relationship you're in is going so well you become suspicious, you think it's too good and something surely must have to go wrong to ruin it all… then suddenly, your worst fears are confirmed and something does go wrong to alter the situation, does that sound familiar? You thought something bad was surely going to happen, so it did, then you say things to yourself like "I told you so, I said this was going to happen and now it has", nobody but YOU did that, YOU bought it on yourself and made it your very own reality, again, using the Law of Attraction in the wrong way.

Chapter 9

Having a Life Plan

Who has a life plan? Well if you do, they can be both a blessing and a curse, let me tell you why. Having a life plan is basically you laying on the line everything you want to achieve in your life and then by what date or how ever old you will be at the time. Having a life plan to a certain extent is a really good thing because it just shows that you're taking control of your life and you know exactly what you want, even if it's not that detailed or specific, its fine, whatever you want you must include in order to be clear of your dreams and wishes. If I'm honest I really hate it when people obsess over life plans and have to complete something by the time they turn 30, then if they don't complete it they think they're a complete failure, again this is really being negative and is no good for your mental health and overall happiness.

By doing this you never get to enjoy what's going on right now in the present and are forever thinking about what you have to do next, no one has said you have to do this, it's just you thinking you have to in order to be a successful person and become more fulfilled, again I could argue this is because you don't have that confidence and happiness within yourself, so you think that if you achieve everything on your list, you'll feel happier and fill the growing void you're desperately trying to fill. Trust me in saying that life can be so stressful and so complicated that you need to make sure you have some fun along the way and open your eyes for a second and take a breath. Again, for busy people this has become a way of life which I completely understand. Some people are complete work addicts and don't even think they have time to spend with their family or have any fun whatsoever, because to them working is the most important thing ever. This really saddens me. Life is so short you really need to ensure you don't take this thing called life so seriously, because in reality all we are is a bunch of cells made up.

Yes, everyone has worries and stresses but like I previously said there are ways of dealing with your busy life to ensure you are happy, you are healthy, and you do have some fun along the way, because you completely deserve to. Have goals, have dreams and have a life plan, just don't be so regimented to sticking with it, because by doing this you could be repelling lots of amazing experiences and people out of your grasp. For example, within your plan before you turn 30, which I don't have but I know some people do, it says you're to work hard to get your career and then will have a relationship after. So, halfway through your training you meet someone who could be really special, but because this would interfere with your plan you don't act on it, see what I mean? You could already be doing this without knowing it, plans and goals are great but please put some room in between for changes and adventures too, because you may spend so much time trying to achieve something that you neglect your own happiness along the way. Then eventually when you do achieve whatever it was within the plan, you may end up realising that it wasn't what you wanted after all… you really don't need to have everything figured out at once, that would be a pretty boring life to me anyway.

Dealing with Relationships

When you're in a relationship with someone you will most likely do anything to please the other person in your relationship, it's so important to not neglect yourself though. When you love someone, you will think about them constantly and will want to spend as much time as possible with them during the earlier stages, usually referred to as the "honeymoon stage". I can see why it's referred to as this, probably because just like an actual honeymoon it's something that appears so exciting and new, which usually it is just that. You need to find that special someone who loves the whole of you, not just the you that's dressed up and wearing makeup. In my opinion a real loving partner will love the very best and very worst version of you, and everything else in between. They should love the you that dresses up but also the you that's got no makeup on and wearing a tracksuit for example, they shouldn't be embarrassed of you when they're in your company, if they are than something is seriously wrong, and you need to address this with your boyfriend / girlfriend as soon as possible. It's sad because I hear of so many examples of relationships that have this problem of acceptance and only being interested when they're wearing a certain item of clothing or doing something they are happy with, that's a recipe for a toxic relationship and is destined for failure in the long run. From what I do know and have experienced I know that the secret to a loving relationship no matter what your age is you both accepting each other for exactly the people you are, without the designer clothes and status symbols or what friends you have. You need to accept the very best and very worst of each other and take into consideration the needs of the other person and vice versa. If you only think about pleasing yourself constantly and putting yourself first, then your partner will begin to feel left out and neglected and will most likely end up leaving you because you failed to acknowledge their needs and wishes because you were too focused on yourself. Remember that love and relationships in general are such a complicated thing, most people live their entire lives trying to figure these kinds of things out but we're not here to judge how people live their lives or what lifestyle choices they have, the most important thing is if you love this person and they love you, LOVE IS LOVE! Don't worry if you don't have a well implemented life plan right now, I certainly don't! My mantra in life has always been I'll do exactly what I want and won't be obsessed with time limits, yes, I want to get married and have a good career, but I don't have exact dates and time scales, when it's meant to happen it will happen... Some people like to have a regimented plan which is completely fine just don't let it consume and rule your life.

Chapter 10

The REAL Recipe for Happiness

One of the most important things I have learnt is that there are only 2 things you need in life in order to be happy. You don't need a fancy car and house to be happy, you don't need a wardrobe full of designer clothes to be happy or anything materialistic that you might think will make you happy, you think they do but actually they only make you happy for that short moment when you acquire them, shortly afterwards this fades away and you're thinking about the next thing you need in order to either fill the invisible void or unhappiness your feeling within your life, I can guarantee.

The first thing out of the two you need in your life to feel confident and happy is SELF-LOVE. I realised that having self-love for yourself is one of the most amazing things. Feeling that love and being happy in your own body and skin and just accepting your flaws and imperfections is the key to happiness, it really is. That saying that says you can't love anyone else until you love yourself is completely true, cliché I know but I now understand this more than ever. The most important person is YOU. Most people neglect this fact and often put other people before themselves, this has to happen sometimes but always remember who the most important person is and who deserves the most happiness and love, it's YOU! I find it so sad when I hear of people who honestly don't love themselves and are constantly putting themselves down and pointing out their imperfections. If this is something you do I can honestly say it's the worst thing you could ever do for your mental health and health overall. If you have this kind of attitude you will carry on attracting this kind of negative energy and negative thoughts to you.

Learn to love yourself like I did. I went a while during a stressful period in my life constantly being angry with myself and constantly putting myself down, it got to the point where I couldn't even look at myself in a mirror without hating what I saw before me, just saying it brings back the memories… I really didn't like looking at my reflection, I felt ashamed and was the furthest I ever could be from self-love. I now love myself more than I ever remember, not in a cocky or arrogant way, just a totally accepting self-love way. I think that's why so many of us don't love who we are, because if we do express the love for ourselves we are labelled as egotistical or being big headed, which isn't the case if you're coming from a pure and authentic place. It's so easy to change your mindset. I started by doing the love yourself challenge I found online.

Go to a mirror look at yourself and get as close to the mirror as you can. Look at yourself and say the following words 20 times each day "I love and accept myself". At first, I can honestly say it felt so weird and strange, but not long after this such a simple and quick exercise dramatically improved things for me and meant I felt so much better about myself, it did take time though. I no longer put myself down or beat myself up the way I used to, it became my normal and I didn't always realise I was being unkind to myself. When I messed up or made a mistake, I learnt from it and then moved on, I didn't get angry with myself or hold a grudge.

So, reader, let me ask you a question to ponder on as you read this book, do you love yourself? It feels weird doesn't it, it feels odd to even think if you love yourself, but let's get out of the mind rubbish of the ego and just think for a second, if you don't love yourself why don't you, and what can you do to change that to start loving yourself for exactly the person you are?

Stage - Two

The second stage I learnt along with having self-love is having SELF-ACCEPTANCE. After you start loving yourself its then time to start accepting yourself and your current situation no matter what it is, remember the current situation you're in won't last forever, that is something which is certain, NOTHING is forever! You need to accept the very person you are, be proud and embrace your personality and embrace and explore your quirks which make you human. This is something I have always lived by, I was always taught by my Mom from an early age that I could be whatever I wanted to be, and I was always accepted, I honestly remember each day how lucky I am and how much it means to me. Never ever, pretend to be something you're not in order to please your partner, friends or family. At the end of the day you're only lying to yourself, again this will mean you live in a negative headspace and will therefore be unable to achieve your dreams and make any sort of progress within your life than the current situation you're in. Again, I hear of so many examples of people who try to be something they're not just to impress an important someone. I vividly remember that I also used to have different versions of myself for different people, usually family members. But then I had a light bulb moment and realised that I could be the very same Jack with every person, if they didn't like it then that was their issue, I wasn't hurting anybody so to me it was their own issue, not mine. When I got to that level of self-acceptance it went further which made me love life even more and meant more and more positive experiences came into my life because people are generally attracted to confidence.

When I say that the only 2 things you need in life in order to be happy are self-love and self-acceptance for yourself is completely true, of course we need relationships and opportunities, but starting with the essentials I feel is key. It's generally known that the people who love themselves for exactly the person they are, are happier and live a longer life.

Chapter 11

We're all Blessed

It's a common fact that as human beings we will always want more, I guess it's just a natural feeling that many people harbor deep within themselves. The key again is to be grateful for every little thing you have within your life. Food, water, your car, home, family, clothes, material items, technology, the air that you breathe, these are all things to be grateful for on a daily basis, I'm repeating this point again because I want it to sink in and hopefully, become second nature. When you're grateful for every single blessing in your life than its impossible to feel depressed, negative, angry or any other negative emotion you may be currently feeling. Feeling these kinds of emotions come from you not realising how many blessings you do have and how much you do have to be thankful for compared to so many unfortunate people in this world who have nothing, but are still happy, funny how it seems to work this way isn't it? If they can be happy while living in a poverty-stricken country and have little or no possessions than we can certainly be overwhelmed with happiness and joy while living in our fast-paced material fused lives.

Several years ago, I travelled to the Gambia with my school for a week of volunteering, what an experience it was. That journey to Gambia just off the coast of West Africa really did change the way I looked at the world around me and changed the way I viewed my own life. I vividly remember being on the plane descending into London feeling a huge amount of joy and happiness. I remember thinking for the first time in my life how happy and thankful I was for living in a modern, developed country, something I had taken for granted my whole life, it really was incredible to feel these kinds of emotions! When many people return from a trip they feel down and depressed when returning to their country and again, take it for granted that their back in their material fused world and lifestyle, what I felt was the complete opposite! I also remember many around me who came on that same trip saying how much gratitude and happiness they felt, even though we were tired and slightly jet lagged, something had changed within us that made us think completely different.

Although that trip was many years ago I still have memories of how lucky I was to travel to a third world country and experience how the people of Gambia lived and the constant smiles on their faces, the hospitality we experienced from them really was second to none, I couldn't have asked for anything else, they would give you the clothes on their back even if they didn't have any more, that's how kind and caring they were. Maybe many of us who are far luckier need to take a leaf out of their book. That feeling of immense gratitude didn't last long though during that time, mentally I just wasn't in a good space and it quickly vanished after returning home, only now looking back do I realise how far I've come and developed, none of this has been overnight, it's a lifestyle choice, I choose to work on my own self-development EVERY SINGLE DAY, why? Because I want to get the best out of my life and cease every opportunity that comes my way, I want to be grateful, I want to inspire others and I want to show you how simple it is to become your best self… it takes a while, it takes consistency, but is it worth it? I think I'll let you answer that for yourself.

<u>Stop Complaining!</u>

This brings me on to the fact that many of us are unhappy in the current situation we find ourselves in. I hear so many times of people saying they're really down and unhappy with the situation there in, be that relationship or work or anything for that matter. Constantly moaning, talking and complaining about it will do NOTHING to help that current situation no matter how much you moan, it's really doing nothing for your mental wellbeing and overall happiness apart from making it worse. If you really want change within your life, no matter how big or small, you really need to WAKE UP to the fact that nothing will change until you allow it to. Maybe you're the type of person that feels inside of you that something is not right, or maybe you feel like you could be living more and enjoying life even more than you currently are. I remember feeling like this and finally waking up to the fact that nothing in my life would change until I allowed it to and becoming the best version of myself, who I'm now striving to be daily. Of course, there may be days when I'm not feeling as good as the last for whatever reason, which is TOTALLY OK, people seem to think if they have the slightest wobble or knock then they've ruined all their hard work and momentum they've been building, which is the total opposite of the truth.

When you finally wake up to the fact that nothing will change until you take the first steps you will then realize how simple it was the whole time. You will finally see what it feels like to be happy and how it feels to be strong and confident and ready for whatever comes your way, almost like an extra layer of protective armor. I feel these feelings all the time now and I can honestly say that its changed my life completely. The old me would never even think in depth like I now do about life, right now you're probably feeling like this makes no sense, just give it some time and see for yourself how AMAZING this process can actually be, just trust me and give it a go.

Chapter 12

It's Never too Late to Change

Always remember, not matter what anyone has told you in the past, it's never too late to change. It doesn't matter who you are, where you've come from, how old you are or even what you've done in the past you can still wake up and become the very best you! I've seen examples of people who were so low and had been in trouble with the law and have still turned their whole lives around and are now completely different people, polar opposites to their former selves. How awesome is that! Someone in particular who has done this is someone who even inspired me, amongst many others, to write this book. Brett Moran completely turned his life around with the power of manifestation, meditation and mindfulness, I urge you to check out his book on Amazon – "Wake The Fuck Up by Brett Moran". To me he represented how much a human can change by just using what they already have within them, going from a criminal to a motivational speaker and life coach is pretty transformative, we can become our own success story with true belief and a lot of determination. I'd also highly recommend you check out Brett's YouTube channel. I've been watching his videos for 3 years now and he views and outlook on life never ceases to amaze me, he's a stunning example of someone who really is living their very BEST LIFE!

<u>Don't be Afraid!</u>

You might be afraid right now to change, you might feel that you won't be accepted by friends and family, you might feel scared and left out if you decide you don't want to do bad things anymore, the list goes on! You need to completely erase these thoughts from your mind, like I said earlier, negative thinking gets us nowhere. It's only our ego doing overtime wanting us to feel this way. Put the ego on mute and look inside your true self for the answer, only then things will become much clearer and happier for you. When I say ego, I ultimately mean all that MESS we hear daily going around our head. Sometimes thoughts of jealousy that someone has more than us, those feelings of self-doubt or feeling insecurities about our appearance etc. Ultimately the ego is all the negativity and controlling thoughts, when you get chance to switch off through meditation or some form of relaxation, only then we can connect to our conscious, the REAL, AUTHENTIC & HONEST bit of our brain that won't be thinking the types of things and limiting / judgmental thoughts that our ego does.

This brings me on to following the crowd. In everyday life many of us feel like we have to do certain things just because everybody else is doing them. It might be drinking down the pub on a Friday night, it might be spending large amounts of time moaning and bitching with your friends, just because they are, so we feel like we have to join in, so we feel cool and relevant. There are so many more examples I could give. We do all of these because some of us feel like we have no choice and we have to, otherwise we won't be accepted and obviously that's the worst thing... isn't it? The simple answer is that NO, this isn't the case. I sometimes wonder that if we all felt we could be whoever we wanted to be and if we all felt like we'd be accepted no matter what, how different would life be? I can bet straight away that all these negative and sometimes damaging patterns just wouldn't happen for the majority of us. We wouldn't be drinking huge amounts of alcohol just to get us through life and we wouldn't be complaining and moaning just to make us feel better, life would be so much more PURE, SIMPLE and HAPPY.

Today especially more and more people do feel this way, because they have woken up and have realised that no one will stop them becoming the best version of them and no one will make them feel down or inferior. I can also add that I no longer feel like I have to do things just to please people, if I genuinely want to do something because it makes me happy then I will, not just to fit in and be accepted, I've never cared about that if I'm being honest…. Well, ever since I decided not to that is! I can honestly say as soon as you decide to change and be who you want you will never look back, ever. Sure, friends may distance themselves and you may in the process realise who is really there for you, although painful I do view this as a good experience because everyone needs to have that moment when they realise who is there for them and who isn't, that's what clarity and truth is. Don't be afraid to show the world the real you, because no one will ever make you be yourself, no one will force you, you've got to make the effort and build up the confidence to show the universe who you really are and the person you want to be, why? Because you owe it to yourself, it's as simple as that.

I never used to understand the saying "the best things in life are free". In a material consumed world, it can be so hard to see how this is the case. It's funny, I can look back now and remember hearing that saying often and always sarcastically laughing and thought to myself and said to others what a load of shit it was. I can hand on heart now say how much I LOVE that phrase; it really is one of my favorites! The simple things in life like nature, having the air that we breathe, where would we be without oxygen? Having a sunrise and a sunset each day. These are all things I never once thought about, I think about them often, because when you really think about it and look up to the stars at night you realise how amazing our universe and world actually is. Again, it's a priceless feeling and made me realise that the very best things in life are free. The feelings within us are also free, feeling self-love for yourself and accepting who you are as a person is again, completely priceless to me and worth more than any materialistic item ever could, it costs NOTHING to be happy, but of course it's true that money does make things easier, but, it only makes us happy to an EXTENT I strongly suggest, yes it makes things easier and much more convenient, but you can wake up tomorrow morning and choose to be happy, happiness is a choice we either make or don't make daily, the latter being the most true for the majority it seems. It's like a trick question asking if you want to be happy, of course you do, tackling multiple areas within your life in lots of small ways will all contribute to this eventually, with time, consistency and belief.

Chapter 13
Sometimes we have to Let Go

Sometimes in life people don't get the hint and want to keep coming back into your life just to remind you they're still there, sound familiar? I've had this problem and it can be a difficult one, especially if they were an important person to you once. This brings me on to cutting contact with someone and how it ultimately can set you free or make you realise something completely different. Deciding to cut all ties and contact with someone will never be easy, trust me, I'm talking from personal experience here I completely know how it feels, and how liberating it can be after it's done. It's harder with family though. Sometimes you need to sit back and think if that said person is good for you, are they benefiting your journey or constantly bringing you down? This isn't something that should ever be taken lightly, it will be clear if it needs to happen, but not always. The thing is though; you don't just decide this overnight. You wouldn't wake up one morning and think *"oh, I don't want this person in my life anymore for no apparent reason",* it comes over time and isn't a decision made lightly.

I'm including this within Being The Best You because this is something within that subject. To be the best you, you have to be completely happy, remove any toxic things from your life, or as much as you can do anyway, sadly, sometimes this includes people. There is never a right time to do it, it will always hurt and not be a nice thing to do. But you must be ready. You need to listen to nobody but yourself. You need to look inside yourself for the answer, you'll find it eventually, it may take longer for others, but it's there. Speak to the individual, explain why you're feeling the way you do, without being petty or personally attacking. Stand your ground and be true to yourself, that is the best advice I can give for this situation. Husband, wife, friend, parent, relative, whoever it is, the same rules apply.

It will feel strange after, but soon after liberating, especially if this person was damaging your life.

What I will say though, is that cutting someone out of your life has to be the last resort. What I have learnt is that ANYONE can change, even when you think they can't, they can, they really can. There is a way back for everyone I believe, but from experience I know that sometimes relationships need to come to an end, from this you'll grow, you may discover you miss this relationship and you want to give it another go, that's totally ok too, there aren't any rules to life and we don't always get it right. You may discover down the line that cutting someone out of your life happened for the best and you feel better for it, just consider and think carefully first. Like the title of the book suggests, it's all about doing what you need to do in order to become and be the BEST YOU.

Removing toxic people can be a scary thing to do because if you've always lived the same way it can seem scary to change. You may have an individual in your life who you know deep down just isn't good for you, you know that they put you down and perhaps stop you from reaching your full potential, but what do you do? My advice is to firstly TALK, one of the simplest acts but always the most effective, not via social media or text or even phone, but good old-fashioned face to face communication. As I said earlier, its articulating to that person why you feel the way you do, by doing this it might even mean your relationship improves and things change for the better, ending the relationship doesn't always have to happen, so do what's best, you deserve to be surrounded by people who lift you up and make you feel good about yourself, you deserve to be in company that makes you feel inspired to tackle your own goals. From experience with the people I now surround myself with I can say for sure that spending time with those who believe in you and celebrate your achievements are the ones to cherish, take note of those who don't applaud when you win, again, examine that a little closer to get to its cause... so many relationships end from jealousy, which is such a waste. Before you move on with reading, I want you to write down who the 5 closest people to you within your life, it might be parents and family, it might be friends, whoever, just write them down. Now, after writing them down next have a think if they make you feel GOOD, HAPPY and are FUN to be around, if several aren't, explore this further, speak to the person and have a think about how this relationship can change into a good one, because your own life experiences and work will and can be affected by those closest to you, that's why I constantly strive to meet and be around people who make me feel good, particularly friends, who I speak about more later on.

Chapter 14

Being Equal

We are all equal. People tend to forget this sadly. It doesn't matter if you're an A list celebrity, a single parent, a millionaire, or a homeless person sleeping rough. All those 4 people are completely different, but all equal and are all worthy. Some people tend to think if you have more money or some sort of "status", then it makes you more important. Bullshit. Everyone deserves to be treated with kindness, understanding, and most importantly, respect. I don't really care if I'm talking to a millionaire or someone on the streets, I'll treat both the same, the homeless person with more compassion, because they deserve it. Most people forget this. When you strip us back to the core, we are ALL humans, literally the same. From a celebrity to an average Joe, we are all worth the same. Money tends to be the thing that changes people, such as social classes and stereotypes. Most people on benefits are seen as violent and not people you'd want to meet. It's just that though, a stereotype. Yes, this may be the case for one or two in life, but not everyone. All people on benefits don't deserve to be painted with the same brush. Most millionaires are seen as snobby and selfish; this may be the case for some but again it's just a stereotype we have basically cooked up in our heads and is completely false.

I've met people from all those 4 categories I spoke about and completely was not the case. Most homeless people had normal lives like me and you, it was sadly down to circumstances out of their control how they ended up the way they did. Some millionaires are so generous and would have time for anyone and again, are just down to earth people who happened to have a dream and act on it, that's why I think so many people are jealous of those who have more than them, don't hate on people, especially those who have worked for it, for achieving their dream and not giving up, maybe people are jealous and judge the way they do because they wish they would have made the effort with their own life.

Judging Others

It comes back to that good old-fashioned saying, "don't judge a book by its cover". To be the best you this is a really important factor, but also a hard one! I still find this hard at times. It's all too easy to see someone and immediately make judgements or assumptions, I guess this can be down to human nature. Most of the time these are wrong, there are definitely occasions where you can be right, but not always. We never really know someone from first impressions, you need to get to know that person, hear their story, it will probably explain a lot.

I'm sure many of you can agree when we see someone in the street dressed a certain way we immediately make a judgement on who that person is, if we think they are nice or not, all based on the clothes they are wearing or the way they walk / act. In some ways I hate this because I'm totally guilty of it, almost like an automatic thing that happens. Take me for example, you may see me wearing an over the top outfit and then make an assumption on me as a person, it could be a compliment or something offensive… but think about it, you actually don't have a clue about me or my life, you don't know anything at all but straight away you're making these assumptions before I've even opened my mouth. So, the point I'm making is that the next time you see someone walking down the street and go to make some sort of judgement, stop yourself and just let them do them and you can do you. Don't beat yourself up either for judging others, it's so embedded in us that we do it DAILY without realising it, it's said that when we meet someone for the first time we make a judgement within the first 30 seconds, that's not very long to make a strong opinion really, is it? I've certainly realised from this in years gone by that we don't always give others enough of a chance, we make the assumption instantly and stick with it, before getting to know them or understanding what they've experienced or been through to make them the way they are. So, next time you're quick to judge someone, take a step back and wait a while, the real version of someone rarely makes an appearance within the first 30 seconds.

Influence

Being influenced, it happens to us daily when you think about it. TV, radio, your friends, family, the increase in social media all contribute to this. We are constantly being fed messages to make us act or behave a certain way. I have never conformed to rule, I guess they broke the mold when they made me! I just don't like being told what to do or how to act, I want to express myself, be creative and live life my own way. Sadly, this really isn't the case for everyone. Many people I've met have felt like they have to act a certain way, just because of a tiny comment someone made, or something they saw in the media. Some people are more sensitive to these things than others, we need to remember that. It's all about being who you want to be, not how the media suggest we act, because that's the "normal" or "correct" thing, or way to behave. Anyway, who is "normal"? What is that word "normal"? If I'm honest I'm not actually sure, I act how I want to behave because for me that's my "normal", you will have your own version, which is completely fine.

It would be so boring if we all acted the same and did the same things. Instead of focusing on what everyone else is doing, focus on what you're doing, what makes you tick and happy. That's another thing! At times people can be so bothered by what other people are doing that they don't get on with their own lives, seriously?! I've witnessed this before. People around you can be so judgmental of your life and constantly obsessed with what you're doing that there not really doing much with their own life. Never live your life through someone else's, you're in the driving seat, not the passenger.

Chapter 15

The "Perfect" Life

There is something crucial you need to realise here. When you look at people's social media, they post photos of their latest purchases, laughing and drinking with friends etc. Do you honestly think that that is their life 24/7? It looks perfect when you look at their profile, maybe too perfect! We only put the good times on our social media. I for one will post celebrations and fun things I'm getting up to, but I won't post about my food shop at the supermarket or the argument I had with someone. All of that doesn't go anywhere near social media. This is the case for most people. The negative or bad parts stay off the internet, the fun happy times do. It's really important to remember to focus on your own life and what you're doing, not being obsessed with someone else's. Try it for yourself, especially if you're currently in a negative headspace because it could really work and change the way you feel. For example, take fun photos with your friends, go for a meal with your family. Post some photos on social media and you yourself will see how lovely and happy it looks.

Try to refrain from being negative on social media and talking about personal matters. I know people that do this. It looks like they're constantly depressed and looking for the drama in their life, clearly not happy people. These people most likely have lots of lovely happy experiences in their life, they just choose to not broadcast it, a complete shame! They keep having bad experiences because currently, that is where their mindset is at. They feel like they can't be happy or even deserve to be, so they focus on the negativity, which makes the situation much worse. Instead, choosing to focus on all the positives in your life and uploading the happy times on your social media will make you seem like a happy positive person, which eventually you will become… trust me.

Just deciding to focus on something positive will instantly lift your mood, I'm not sure of the exact science of it but that's how the Law of Attraction works. For example, some people say a hug will instantly make them feel better. Human contact can actually do this, there's no exact reason as to why but a hug has been scientifically proven to lift the mood and make us feel more positive. The social media example is important to change in order to be happy, stop stalking that person's social media profile, being obsessed with what they do next. While you're putting all your energy into this you could be focusing on your life and what fun things and experiences YOU want to do next. Just another tip in order to become the BEST YOU. It's like when you think of a lawn of grass, sometimes we can become so obsessed and interested in someone else's grass that we take zero care of our own, we don't notice it started to wilt and turning brown, all the while feeding the other persons... by doing this we're NEGLECTING ourselves in the process, we're caring too much about someone else's next move without making any of our own, when really we deserve nothing more than our own attention.

Self-Care

Taking care of YOU is another important step for any healthy life and becoming the best you. So many of us today lead busy lives, it can become the norm to skip breakfast, constantly rush from place to place without thinking about ourselves and how we're currently feeling. Most people I've come across in my life will come up with the excuse that they're too busy to care about their appearance, too busy to care about their diet and too busy to care full stop! Really!? Having this sort of attitude certainly won't get you anywhere, that's why the majority of people complain about being tired all the time, even though they sleep each night they still feel tired and sleepy throughout the day. This is all down to how you sleep and how you relax. I can remember and look back on a time when I used to sleep but then wakeup and still feel tired and still feel stressed, it was literally like my brain would refuse to turn off, no matter how hard I tried. This was years before I discovered mindfulness and the Law of Attraction. Does this sound familiar for you in your own life? Self-care shouldn't just been seen as a popular trend, because ultimately it's a lifestyle choice, making time for you and ensuring you have a healthy wellbeing is the kindest act you could carry out, it isn't selfish, it isn't self-absorbed and it isn't disregarding everyone else's feelings whilst doing it, it's giving yourself the kindest gift that every single one of us deserves.

Chapter 16
Putting YOU First

The answer to this one people is really pretty simple… just MAKE time for yourself! My Mom for example is a really great example with this one (sorry Mom!). Being a single parent, she had to be constantly there for me and my twin sister, she really didn't get much time for herself. She would probably argue that she still doesn't get loads… that's probably down to me thinking she's my personal chauffeur to take me wherever I want, oops! Sometimes it's about making time. I've had so many people say things like *"I don't bother about myself"* or *"I don't care if I go without"*, be honest with yourself, do you care, really? Just saying that statement might not seem it, but it really is a negative thing to say. When you analyze it you're basically saying that you don't give two shits about yourself.

I'm saying the above because this was basically what I used to say. I put so much energy into other people that I stopped caring about myself and my needs. I would constantly be tired from over working at College. I even remember saying when I found out I got into university that I *"didn't deserve a party"* when my family offered to throw me one, for some reason I was in such a bad place mentally that I didn't think I deserved to have loved ones congratulate me or give me a card. I thank god, every single day that I was able to wake up and actually become someone I'm now proud to be. I can look in the mirror and feel love for who I am.

So, take my advice with that, even if it's just baby steps. Maybe dedicate one single hour to yourself when you're not so busy with work and other commitments, like at a weekend perhaps. Do something that you and you alone want to do, not something that your children or spouse will enjoy, something that you will enjoy without thinking about everyone else for once. Thinking about other people really is an amazing thing, it makes you a good person and the complete opposite of being selfish. But too much and it can go the wrong way, like it did with me. Maybe you could read that book you've been meaning to read for a while, maybe visit a friend who you've been too busy to see for ages and have a coffee. Who cares as long as it's something YOU want to do, that's all that matters.

It's funny, writing this book I originally wanted to help others but as I'm currently writing this and reading through it's giving me so much inspiration and happiness… just reading through my own advice gives me such a warm feeling inside. It really is a pleasure for me to give you, whoever you are, this advice. As you carry on reading just absorb the information, don't think too hard and don't judge yourself too quickly. This isn't me trying to lecture you, so please don't feel like it is. This is me just giving honest and genuine advice of what I think, that's all. You don't have to agree with everything I've said, this is just the advice of one person out of how many billion we have living on earth. All I'm asking is that you at least CONSIDER it, you may have your own reasons as to why you don't agree with points I might have raised, within life generally you won't always have people who see your side of things or agree with your way of thinking, what I say is this, as long as you're happy and not harming anyone in the process, THINK how you want to think and BE who you want to be.

Vibes are Real

When you're in a certain environment it really can have a huge impact on your overall mood and how you're feeling. When people talk about "energy" and "vibes" there really is truth related to it. Try it yourself and you will quickly realise how REAL energy is and how it can make you feel inside. For example, I've previously walked into a shop, I can't remember exactly what shop, but I just remember straight away getting this really odd feeling, I can't really describe it. It basically felt like something was off and not quite right, I left and felt better once I had. This people is ENERGY. Clearly someone in there was in a bad mood or just wasn't putting a very positive energy out. Try this next time you're out and see what kind of vibes and energies you can feel. Sometimes I walk into a place and it feels so warm and inviting, this doesn't even need to be people laughing and joking, it could literally be an empty space. Something about it feels good and positive, again the opposite could happen. Sometimes I visit places and feel nothing, zero. This is absolutely fine because sometimes there's just no connection, no good energy but also no bad energy. That previous statement on energy might sound completely wacky but trust me and try it for yourself next time you're out. Energy ultimately isn't physical, it's a feeling, I'm at a point now where I can't help but feel it, I feel it when I meet people, I'm sure you've also experienced that situation where you meet someone and you click straight away, you connect on a much deeper level, I have many friendships like this that are truly priceless.

Chapter 17

Love your Home

Environments in general can have a real impact on your overall happiness, attitude, and energy levels. Think about where you live, do you feel happy? Do you feel like you can relax and have fun? If you answer no to any then it's time to implement some simple changes in order to get your positivity and energy levels back on track. It's never too late for ANYONE. Simple changes like having a huge spring clean and de-clutter of your bedroom would be a good place to start. It's been proven that living in clutter can have a negative impact on your overall mental health and happiness. Having piles of clothes on the floor of your bedroom would be an example of this. When you think about your happiness levels and overall attitude you probably wouldn't think that the amount of clutter clogging up your home could be a contributing factor... but it really is. Buying some lavender room spray or scented candles to burn in your living room on a night could also help, it really is whatever works for you. The place you're in the most be that your house, workplace or anywhere else needs to be a positive environment, otherwise it will completely have a knock-on effect when it comes to your overall attitude and how you then deal with everyday situations. If your most used environment is a place where you feel comfortable then congratulations, these steps don't apply to you!

Home is the place where you should feel most happy when you arrive back after a long day of work, where you can relax and be your TRUE self. I've heard of many people in the past who can't be themselves at home, they can't do the things they want to do, this saddens me so much and I really think that if you can't be yourself in your own home then where can you be? There isn't a one size fits all answer for this one. If the above is something you can relate to you need to have a think about why you feel like this. If the reason why you don't like your home is more because of the physical environment, such as a certain room or space you don't like it's about thinking of little changes to implement in order for you to become more comfortable. You could spend time re-decorating a certain space, it doesn't have to cost the earth to give your bedroom or other space a mini makeover, try upcycling, visit a charity shop or a car boot for some inspiration. Giving a room or space a change physically is sure to make you feel much better mentally when you've spent time working on it and making it a pretty space for YOU, remember, that's the word I will use the most throughout this book because it's not about being the best family, the best partner or the best parent, it's about being the best YOU, it's what you can do and change in order to become a better version, everything I've referenced thus far all relates to this overarching theme.

Chapter 18
Putting It into Action

Think it, **believe it**, **work for it, achieve it!** As cringe as that may sound you have to realise that this is how it works, it's so simple, it's not rocket science and I believe it can be applied to almost any situation. Just give it a try for yourself again now. I think it's best to start with something simple, then try it and you can let me know that it's worked for you. Let's say you've seen a dress you really like but right now you can't afford the price. Let's try the formula. Write it down on your manifestation list… remember the thing I mentioned earlier? Daily I want you to think about it and then go one step further and visualize yourself wearing that dress or whatever it is, it doesn't even need to be a material item. Believe, believe that you'll somehow manage to afford it, even if you don't actually know how right now, that doesn't matter, it doesn't matter how you'll achieve anything in life, we spend so long thinking to ourselves how and why, you don't always need to have the answers to everything, that's coming from someone who loves to always be in control and have it all figured out, but sometimes it's about taking a little leap into the unknown. Work for it, not always the easiest of steps I know but think long & hard about what it is you can do in order to get the dress, to ger whatever you want… persistence is key, don't take no for an answer, in the long run it will be more than worth it. Finally, Receive it, it will happen, if you think about it daily and ASK the universe eventually something will happen which will result in you getting it. It might have a price reduction; this is something that's happened to me before. It's such a great feeling when you realise that all that waiting paid off and you can finally have the thing you've been obsessing over for ages. You might get an advance on your wages, win some money on a scratch card, realise you have more money in your bank account than you thought, all these are examples of what could happen when it comes to the fourth step of achieving what it was that you constantly thought about. I can't put a time on this, it could take 1 week or 1 month or anything in between or even longer, the fact is that it WILL WORK eventually. Don't try doing it with an attitude that just expects it to happen there and then straight away, guess what, it WONT WORK, you need to have an attitude of believing that it will. If you do the steps but keep believing in the back of your head or subconsciously that it won't work than it won't, it's that simple. Again, you can't sit on your ass either waiting for it to happen, very rarely will anyone come to you, it's YOU who has to put the effort in and make it a reality, the moment you fully realise that is when real change will begin to occur.

Trust me when I say that once you've tried this there is no going back. If someone had told me 3 years ago when I first started typing up notes that I'd be writing a book with the aim of inspiring or motivating others I wouldn't have believed them, it's as simple as that. Do you know why? Because I wasn't motivated myself and thought all that positive stuff was a load of crap, funny to think I used to make fun of positive quotes that actually make a whole heap of sense.

Sometimes it seems like people enjoy being negative, like why? Life is so bloody short that there really isn't time to spend bitching and moaning about the weather, like, come on people we live in England so get over it already! No but on a serious note, if we all calculated how much time a day, week, month or year we spend being negative it would probably add up to quite a big amount… if we turn that the opposite way and calculate the time we spend being positive, lifting people up and inspiring others it would probably be quite little for some and a lot for others.

Chapter 19

Goal Setting is Crucial

GOALS, DREAMS and WISHES – it's so important to have all 3 of these. Without them I think life would be really dull and boring – you need these things to stop you from stagnating, remember I mentioned that word earlier on? Goals give us something to look towards, make them realistic when you set them, otherwise you may not be as inclined to work towards them, this is really important. Be that professional or personal ones, goals are important, and it feels so amazing when you get to say you've achieved one. That's something I do constantly, and it really works – I think it gives you more motivation when you see something written down, it just makes you want to achieve it. Write down your goal and put the paper where you'll see it every single day until the goal is achieved and can be ticked off your list. That should take a grand total of 5-10 minutes out of your day. Some people recommend you do huge lists full of goals. For me this can actually feel quite overwhelming so each month I write down my 5 goals for that month, that way it's a good number of goals for me to work on. I've been doing this for almost 3 years and enjoy looking back at the goals at the end of the month and ticking them off my list. A fair few times I haven't achieved a goal on my monthly list, that's absolutely OK. I either add it to my next month's list or decide I no longer need to focus on it. So, don't see that as a failure, instead focus on the things that YOU have achieved.

I write each of my goals down, then below I write down the important stuff – how I plan on doing it. Make sure you write a few notes down below on any details you know about how you're planning on doing this. Then at the end of each month I sit down again and write a little about how the past month has been and how many of the goals I managed to achieve. When you're reading this book have a look at the date, if it's coming to the end of a month or the beginning of a new one go and spend a good 20 minutes having a think of 3-5 realistic goals you want to achieve throughout the next month. Then make plans below on what you'll do, where you'll go, who you'll ring in order to achieve it and tick it off you list. It's the best feeling ticking them off and marking them as done I promise you; you'll love this exercise. Doing this means that I'm constantly on the ball and forever improving on myself – it's certainly dedication but why wouldn't you want to take the time, remember, the best project you'll EVER work on is YOURSELF!

For me when I write a goal, I'm a strong believer that you can't think too big. For the first few years of my goal setting journey I'd set really simple and achievable ones, ones that in the back of my head I knew I'd achieve anyway, it was still a good exercise, but I knew I could challenge myself more. Now I write goals with ambition behind them, I want to challenge myself and push myself to the limit, because I know just what's possible and what can be achieved when you put your mind to it. Also, I sometimes set goals for the year which are much bigger which gives me a focus and something to work towards, it's all about what works for you. I know many people that don't write goals but still achieve and get a good amount out of life, its more about finding what works for you and doing it that way. Another practice I like to use is using steppingstones, for me this is underneath each goal where I said I write down how I'm going to achieve it, breaking this down I include 3-5 or more smaller steppingstones that describe the steps I need to take in order to achieve my goal. Sometimes it can be overwhelming, so having each step broken down into mini chunks is much more effective I feel.

<u>Dreams</u>

Dreams are next! Let's turn those dreams into reality, shall we? It's about time you take those dreams out of your head and actually give them sounds, colour, smells, gravity – make them REAL. We all have dreams and again, it's healthy to have them and to believe in something so special is truly wonderful. I know many people and we see many success stories daily of people who have had their dreams become true, have you? It could be having children, getting married, landing that dream job or just simply losing some weight so you feel confident again.

Dream charts are a great thing for that. These charts are realistic and break down those thought barriers to actually give some substance to your dreams and make them possible. Remember that banned word we're not allowed to say, it actually says I'M POSSIBLE but backwards – always remember that one, it's almost like it was intended to say that… I wonder! Many templates are available online, but you can easily make one yourself, with a pen and paper you're good to go. When I make dream charts, I'm someone who enjoys looking at visuals like photos, rather than just text describing what I want.

Let me give you some inspiration so after you've read this chapter you can get started on creating one for yourself. Throughout this book when you come across any tips I give I urge you to stop reading and complete the task, then you can continue reading further. That way you're learning along the way and implementing some of the advice I give. Back to the example. For years I suffered with low self-esteem and bad confidence, I just didn't have belief in myself which meant I would isolate myself and didn't really make an effort to meet new people, I just didn't have an interest. I'd look at others around me who had large groups of friends and dream of having the same, all I wanted was to have people who loved and accepted me for me. I dreamt for so long to have just a nice group, it didn't have to be lots, but a few close friends would be nice.

Fast forward 5 years later and the change is transformative, I have more real and true friends than I ever could have imagined having, they all influence my life in different ways and it really is incredible. It could be anything, maybe you want a loving relationship, a car, a new career, it could literally be anything, no dream is too small, and no dream is too big… what are your dreams? So many of us grow up having lots of dreams, especially as children, we spend time talking about them and feel proud in telling adults what our dreams and desires are. But then, everything stops. When we get older we gradually hear people stop talking about their dreams, they stop having the passion they did as a child, it's almost like that when we get to a certain age we feel like we can't dream, we can't have wishes, like it's the stuff of fairy tales. However, it's not, YOU are allowed to dream, YOU are allowed to wish, and YOU are allowed to want more, YOU deserve more. So, make a vision board, make a dream chart, if you haven't vocalized your dreams before then start, start telling people where you want to go, who you want to meet and the person you want to become, because life won't and isn't waiting for you, the only person who has the control and power to change anything is YOU. I'm suggesting multiple ideas and practices to you throughout this book, but if you don't get up and act on them then nothing will happen, it's down to you and you alone.

Chapter 20

Wish Upon a Star

Wishes, the best kind, you certainly can't have enough wishes. This one makes me think of when it's your Birthday and you're asked to blow out the candles and make a wish. Instead of just doing it on your Birthday it should be done every single day, why not, it's fun and gets you thinking and inspired about what you truly want. A lot of the time people are told to not be selfish and to think of others when they wish for something, that's a good thing to do but let's forget about that for a moment. Sometimes it really pays to think about yourself and what YOU want. You need to start with number 1, whoever says it's selfish to think about yourself probably say that because in society we're made to think it's selfish to treat ourselves, do the things that we truly want to do and to god forbid, be happy with who we are. Wouldn't it be amazing if everyone lifted each other up and made each other feel great about themselves? We should start a revolution or group full of genuinely happy and positive thinking people, think about all the good that could happen!

Wish for whatever you like, wishing rocks are something I use constantly for a multitude of things. I started off with a basic rock I found on a beach, then you can cleanse it with salt water which basically means all existing energy, particularly if it was negative is washed away and is ready for whatever energy you decide to put towards it… make it positive, especially if you're dedicating the time to do a few of these exercises I'm recommending. I also do another simple exercise which will take you approximately 30 seconds. Put the rock somewhere you can easily reach it each night when you get into bed, I put mine on a bedside table. Pick it up and think about the very BEST part of your day. If nothing special has happened on your day think a little deeper… it could be that your train or bus was on time instead of being delayed, that you watched your favorite show or had a delicious meal. It could be that you had fun catching up with friends or if you've had a day full of negativity, I always use the one statement that you can ALWAYS rely on… just saying you're lucky to be alive and living. Have fun trying this, doing it on a night at the end of your day is also awesome because you get to do a mini review of the whole of your day whilst picking your best bit.

Also, don't worry if you don't have the time to dedicate to do all of these exercises, there are many times when I'm busy with university or jobs where I don't even have time to meditate and have left it a few days before. It doesn't mean you're not being positive or passionate about being the person you want to be. Sometimes doing less of the exercises but putting the time into the ones you do choose to do will work even better for you and have a stronger effect after practicing them for a while. For me most of these exercises have become a part of my daily life and I can't really imagine my life without them – it's made my life so much better and healthier, both physically and mentally. Remember when you start getting mentally stronger your physical health will start improving. I remember hearing a story about a man who was dying with cancer and started improving when he started practicing the Law of Attraction and positive thinking… how can this be possible though? There are multiple scientific claims about the Law of Attraction which I won't even bother going over, there far too complicated and don't make much sense! Basically, like I said before, like attracts like. Focusing on the fact that you're going to be alright, even if you feel you won't be. What feels better, thinking you're going to be alright and having positive thoughts or thinking that you won't be… it's not going to do any good for your physical health, mental health and energy levels. I have so much more physical energy now than I ever used to, nothing much physically has changed but because the mental strength has got stronger and stronger it's had an effect on all my health. Most of this is free too, just see me as your personal trainer, not in the gym but your positivity personal trainer! These exercises are like actual exercises, instead of it being for your body it's for your mind muscles, the most important to train and keep healthy for your overall wellbeing.

Chapter 21

Are YOU Feeling More Positive Yet?

So, are you all still with me? I hope you find this book a guide of tools and exercises you can use whenever you feel you need that little dose of inspiration. When I've been writing each section, I've found myself getting motivated from things I've previously said... how funny is that? I think it shows that no matter how positive you are you always need that little pick me up to make you realise how amazing this world we live in is. We're all just tiny fish in an absolutely huge pond. We all lead different lives, have different jobs / careers, some have families, and some don't, but everyone is basically the same when you think about it. Ladies out there, there's no difference between you or Beyoncé, celebrities are still people they just have a public image and probably spend more money than we could ever think about monthly to keep up their appearance. What I'm trying to say is about how we compare ourselves to others, it's probably one of the easiest things we could ever do, but also the most damaging. I think everyone has done this at some point in their lives, some more so than others. I used to do this so much and it can get quite depressing, especially when it comes to social media, it can be both a blessing and a curse when it comes to fueling someone's positivity. I think like everything in life, it depends on how you use it. I use it to look at what other people are doing and take inspiration from it, not look and feel jealous and then feel negative about my own self, that's what can happen sadly.

Yes, I am bringing up social media again, I want this stuff to stick my darlings! We ultimately use social media to paint a pretty picture of our "perfect" lives and selves. Trust me, social media can be such a good tool but it's important to not compare yourself to others, you need to stop searching for perfection, just be YOU, just do YOU, and be the honest and perfect YOU.

As soon as you stop comparing yourself to others you can focus on loving yourself for who you really are. I'm probably repeating myself here but trust me, no good comes from constantly comparing yourself to others, it could be your own friends, family, work colleagues, just stop, because it really won't achieve much, apart from making you feel worse and less complete in the long run. It's like people look at others and wish they could lead the life they are living, although you probably don't believe it, the truth is that you CAN, you can do everything anybody else is doing and more, it's such victim territory when we compare, because straight away we're coming in with the mindset that we feel that person or life is so far out of reach we won't be able to achieve it. Take inspiration from others, yes, there will always be people with more than you but there will also always be people with less too, so stop comparing, just stop. With comparing I think it's human nature to do it, I still feel myself looking at what others are either wearing or doing and then look at myself and almost compare myself to them. Luckily these days I'm quick to snap out of it and realise that I'm on my journey, and they are on theirs. I don't need to be asking why I'm not doing the same because it doesn't matter how close you are with someone; each journey is different because we ALL have different goals and ambitions that we're looking to achieve.

Are YOU Feeling More Positive Yet?

Chapter 22

My Journey So Far

So, I guess it's time to go a bit more in depth on what I've referenced previously throughout, a little about my own journey so far and how I come to tell you what I'm telling you in this book. If someone had told me 3 years ago that I'd be writing a book about inspiration and motivation I'd have laughed in their face, literally! I guess at the moment in time I just wasn't at that point of even thinking like that. I had habits, like we all have, the problem is that they were negative and looking back, mentally quite destructive. Coming out as gay a few years prior to this and finally being open and honest about who I am definitely had a part to play in it. After I first came out in 2014, I was pretty happy, I felt like I was happy to finally say it, I guess I was far from accepting it. It wasn't until early 2016 that I finally started to be the real me – the thing I was searching for was staring me in the face and I had no idea. Because I wasn't being myself and wearing a mask it ended up making me feel so much worse. If anyone has ever overcome something similar in the past, you'll know what I'm getting at. You don't see the damage you're doing to yourself in that very moment. It's only after when you're looking from the outside in that you actually realise what's been happening.

This alongside general / social anxiety contributed to me basically feeling pretty shit daily. For people that aren't very close to me this will probably be a shock, I always seemed so happy and energetic, oh if only that was the case, sadly, it wasn't. I think a lot of it is also down to your habits. I'd always been the same in terms of thinking negatively, almost pushing the self-destruct button on my own life, how weird is that? I can't really give one reason as to why, but I just wasn't happy, there was something deep inside of my body that was bursting to get out and escape… that was me, the real me. The other me was simply a mask, an image I'd portray in order to seem "normal" and to fit in with the crowd. Again, doing this is so damaging and was doing ZERO for my mental health, looking back on it now I don't even recognise that version of myself, in a very strange way I'm happy it happened. With the habits I do feel I was a sheep, like many of us are, until I eventually woke up. I would be suspicious instantly if anything good happened to me, I'd say things like *"oh, it's just too good to be true"*, does that sound familiar for anyone else?

The beliefs I had for so long grew into belief systems, these were statements I knew were totally true and were ingrained from me believing them for so long, most of them were damaging and stopped me from growing at all as a person. I didn't enjoy life at all, I didn't really care too much either, I didn't work hard, and I wasn't too interested in much, it was a strange time but one that I experienced and went through, and more importantly, SURVIVED. It's funny because while I was in this state, I was constantly searching for happiness, it was always externally, in material objects, and sometimes people. What I didn't realise and only can see now years later that the whole time everything I was craving and looking for I possessed INSIDE OF ME, everything I needed was in ME, not in external material objects, not in clothes, not in food and comfort eating, just me as a person, as imperfectly perfect as I am. When you realise that everything you need to be happy is within you, it's so eye opening and changes everything for the better. Right now as you're reading this you can be the best version of yourself because it already exists, its already in you but sometimes the fog in our mind can be so thick we just can't see it, we can't see the beauty and light within, but it's there, it's in ALL of us, no matter who you are or what bad or awful things you've done, it's still there, it always was.

I also think that when dealing and looking at the bad things we've done and the hardships we've experienced, it's about letting them go, because if we let them go, they can't hurt us anymore, the past is the past and as much as we want we can't change it. When we let go of the past like that it's much more positive then holding on to it. I could look at the very short time in my life in 2 ways. I could feel bitter that I felt the way I did and angry with the space I was in, or let it go and feel thankful that in the grand scheme of things, it was for a pretty short period of time and ever since I've been able to explore my personality in ways I could have only imagined a few years back. Holding grudges get us nowhere, that's why I say I'm happy it happened. I mentioned earlier in the book about letting go of toxic people, that's another thing that had to take place for me to get to the space I'm in now. Yes, these exercises can be beyond scary, we all hate confrontation and dealing with issues that may have been affecting us for some time, maybe even years. But without dealing with them they will carry on affecting, carry on making you feel miserable. Deep down, you know what the right thing to do is.

Now I'm the happiest I've been in my whole life, I honestly feel like a completely new person and have so many healthy practices / exercises in my life, I have every faith in myself and I can actually outload say that I'm proud of MYSELF, I'm proud to be ME. Can you say these statements? Are you too embarrassed to say them? Just try it, it honestly feels priceless. As I said earlier, most people are probably more used to insulting and degrading themselves that it eventually becomes "normal", paying yourself a compliment would probably make you feel weird or embarrassed because you're just not used to doing it. The more you do it the more natural it will feel… find a quiet space and try it, I promise it's not crazy.

I was bought up by a single parent since the age of 6, my Dad left the family home and we had a damaged relationship in the years that followed. Several years ago, I decided to cut contract with him, things just weren't working, I don't want to go into lots of detail, but I want to be totally honest with what I've experienced, especially if it can help others. I needed those years apart from him to find myself and discover who I was. Recently I decided I wanted a relationship with my Dad again, it was the missing piece in the puzzle and after learning everything I had about forgiveness and letting go of the past, I knew that even my Dad could change. So, no, my life has been far from perfect but I'm still proud of it all. Currently, although I have expressed to my Dad I'd like to give things another go, he isn't quite ready, and honestly, that's totally ok. We're all human, we all have emotion and I'm a big believer that when its meant to be it will happen, I have a hope that in the future me and my Dad will have some sort of reconciliation, because I know from what I've experienced thus far, just about anything is possible.

What Worked for Me

I've previously had counselling twice for general anxiety and PTSD, and it did work but nothing has helped more than the general acceptance that I now have for myself. I'm not ashamed to be 100% honest with you. I did used to feel not worthy, I did USED to feel constantly unhappy, no matter what I did nothing seemed to be working. I did used to hate myself and even saw myself entering the stages of self-harm. I don't like talking about that time too much because of the intense upset it caused, however, getting to a stage where I wanted to physically harm myself was literally the biggest wakeup call I have ever been given, it was like an outer body experience of me saying to myself… *"Jack, what the hell are you doing?"*.

From that point onwards and over time, things changed, gradually and little by little, certainly not overnight, it's been a long road but once I'm glad to have walked, because I've discovered a lot about myself along the way. I also started watching YouTube videos on self-love, meditation and mindfulness. The following motivational speakers have helped me drastically, I enjoy watching these videos or audio books and listening to what advice they recommend. The first is Brett Moran who I mentioned earlier, next is Jack Canfield, an American author and motivational speaker who has published many best-selling books including the *"Success Principles"*, to name just one. The third is Bob Proctor, at the grand age of 83 he is another hugely successful motivational speaker & author and has previously written books such as *"You Were Born Rich"* to name just one. He teaches people how to manifest exactly what they want into their lives. Another good book to note is the one that started this all off, *"The Secret"* written by Rhonda Byrne, an Australian TV producer and writer. This along with The Secret film that includes many motivational speakers, including Bob Proctor, will completely change how you think. The film can be bought via Amazon to download on your TV & tablet to watch, along with ordering the book.

Along with this I read books by the brilliant Ferne Cotton, what a national treasure she is. I like how raw and real her books are that speak about happiness and touch quite a bit on her own experiences of dealing with mental health whilst being a parent and living in the spotlight, *"Happy"* and *"Calm"* are just two of the ones currently available.

Chapter 23
Experiences

It's hard because it's not nice thinking about the hard times, it's not nice going there. BUT, in order to finally free yourself from the ageing mind bullshit you HAVE to go there, you need to think and understand why this issue or memory, or situation made or still makes you feel the way it does... otherwise it will stay there, and it won't budge. The only person you're hurting is YOU, not the person or situation that's holding you a prisoner in your OWN brain. How is that even fair? How is that even allowed? Just remember something next time something similar arises: YOU control your brain; your brain DOES NOT control you! Sometimes it seems like the 2nd statement is true for some people, it's time to retake charge and tell it who the real master is! Why is it we feel that we're a slave to our own minds, like it's the unspeaking master that we must abide by, your thoughts are YOUR CHOICE, it's your choice to think positively, it's your choice to think negatively... just read that statement again and really digest it, it's our choice to think each individual thought each day, your friends and family or anybody else doesn't make you think a certain thought, it's down to YOU and YOU alone.

I know when things aren't going well I can appreciate that it isn't easy to look on the bright side of life, trust me I've been there a lot so I understand that when you're in a certain headspace, it can feel near impossible to think from a positive one. However, I do feel it's more the way we react to what happens to us is the real defining factor, it's not really about what happens, it's about how we respond and act and move forward after. We can't stop bad things happening to us, I can't stop someone upsetting my day, but then I could argue that I let them, especially if I let it consume me and have a knock-on effect, if I reacted differently maybe it wouldn't have ruined my day. With everything this won't work of course, somethings will happen that are just totally shit and that's it, but I do feel the way we react to life situations can have a massive impact on what happens next.

I'm no one special, I'm just someone that hopes to inspire and motivate others no matter your age, where you live, your sexuality, religion, gender, how much money you have or don't have, job or anything else that could ever define a person. You're never too old to change. You could be 99 years old with hours to live and decide that today is the day you're going to change and be the person that you've ALWAYS wanted to be. That's a dramatic example but there really isn't any excuses or reasons you could give!

Experiences and learning curves, we need these to grow, evolve, change and become stronger and sometimes, better people. Some people just bob through life gently doing the same things, visiting the same holiday destinations and working at the same place for their whole life or years at a time, this might work for some people but it sure as hell doesn't work for me! Everyone is different, but for me I like change, I used to be scared of change but then I learnt to embrace it. I realised that the reason I was scared of change was due to the fact that I was worried about doing something new, worried about meeting new people, would I fit in? Would I manage? This definitely wasn't very healthy for me in the long run, I started to take leaps of faith and jump in headfirst without wearing the armbands. I could have drowned, but I didn't, I came back up to the surface stronger than ever. These days I embrace change however I can, with the people I meet, how I spend my free time, the clothes I wear etc. I like to be different; I like to not be the norm and I never conform to what a "normal" person is supposed to be.

Change CAN Be a Good Thing

I'm looking at the subject of change because mentally it's extremely important in order to test yourself and realise just how much you're capable of. Trust me when I say you're much more capable of many things you haven't done yet, you just need to take that small leap of faith into the water and give it a go. You might enjoy it more than you could ever have imagined, or you might realise that from doing it it's not for you and actually? You'd be suited to something much more different. Just give it a go…. What's the worst that could actually happen? That's something else we as humans like to do, expect the worst ALL of the time, god it must get so exhausting for some people that are constantly fearing the worst will happen or looking for the negatives in a situation. Going back to the Law of Attraction, if you go into a situation looking for the negative than you will DEFINITELY find it. The same with if you go into a situation looking for a bit of positive, even if it seems "impossible" you will honestly find it, you just need to trust me and give it a try! That's why I put "impossible" in inverted commas, remember, that word isn't in your vocabulary anymore!

Doing new things has been one of the biggest things on my journey which has changed me for the better, self-love and acceptance being the number 1 highest. I did something not so long ago that I would never have dreamed of doing, in general it was so out of character for me and entailed some amazing experiences which have made me grow so much. I taught groups of 15-17 years old's for a summers through a programme called The Challenge ran by NCS, what an incredible experience it was, I never once thought a few years back I'd have the confidence to stand in front of teenagers, there's no way! I remember telling family members that I wanted to do it again, some were shocked, I think I shocked myself if I'm completely honest. Once I completed the experience, I remember thinking to myself *"wow Jack, you really CAN do whatever you put your mind to, ANYTHING is possible."* It really was empowering and made me realise that nothing was out of reach, not if you truly want to give it a go and if you're willing to put in 100% effort to get it without sitting on your ass, then you'll get there eventually… honest!

That's why I said, doing the same things constantly we do without really thinking. It's habits, we all have them, and we have to have them for routine and some form of normality. I'm not saying to completely give up on all your current habits and routines, I'm just asking you to shake it up a bit and give something new a try, it's a mantra I try to stick to each month and experience 1 new thing, activity or place. You could perhaps learn a new hobby, learn a new language or learn to cook a new dish that you'd never dream of usually tackling. Why wouldn't you dream of doing it, scared of "failing" perhaps? That's another word I really try to not use, I admit it can be so hard at times! Instead of saying you "failed" let's say that it didn't work this time or things didn't go to plan or it wasn't suited to you, or ultimately, you LEARNT. Those statements definitely don't sound as bad as the word "failed", do they?

We ALL make mistakes, we ALL have slip ups, because we're HUMAN it doesn't matter who you are or how intelligent you may be, just remember, you're ALLOWED to make mistakes and quit if something isn't suiting you. We only have 1 life, so why should you have to be suffering doing something that you just don't want to be doing? I certainly wouldn't, if your heart isn't 100% in it, maybe have a think about why that is, only YOU can answer that one – as long as YOU'RE 100% honest with yourself. So, what's the worst that could happen… we get lost and end up finding ourselves? Because that's what happened to me, yes, I got lost, I never thought I'd find anything again, but after a lot of work on rewiring my mind I did find myself, not the Jack that was there before though, a much BETTER one, a refreshed and renewed one, that's why I developed the title I did, because from experiencing what I did it made me realise that I was never being even half of the best me I could, I knew that probably a lot of others also aren't being the best version they could be, again, which is usually down to the experiences we face or the setbacks we experience, it's easy to give up hope, but this is why I'm giving you this message in the form of this book, to tell you that no matter how bad you might be feeling, you can change everything around, I'm living proof of just what's possible.

Chapter 24

Are You Stagnating?

Going back to earlier when I talked about stagnating as a person, like when water in a pond gets old and just isn't fresh, vibrant and ALIVE anymore. If you're reading this it stands a good chance you're alive, right? Let's start acting like it then, shall we? Doing new things does just that, visit a new city, apply for a new job if you feel like your current one has reached its sell by date, just think LOGICALLY first if that's viable, suitable for you and something that you actually want to do. The very best bit about doing something new is how ALIVE it makes you actually feel; I still get those butterfly's in my stomach and slightly anxious feeling when I work somewhere different or meet a new group of people, it's not a feeling of a bad anxiety it's the very opposite. It feels exciting and a feeling that will never get old for me. It's far better than knowing exactly what's going to happen every day, 7 days a week, I know which feeling I'd rather have, do you?

Throughout the reading process of my book I want you to put it down for a few days or weeks at a time, some of this stuff is quite deep and heavy, take some time to read some of my content, then go away and have a think about how it makes you feel, if it makes you consider doing something different or making some changes. If it does than that's pretty awesome and only a bonus for me of writing this book. If it doesn't have any effect on you than that's also totally fine, there's no right or wrong answer, some people might be perfectly happy as they are and already feel like there being the person they want to be, if that's you, then a huge congratulations because these days that can seem to be a minority of people. Welcome to the club, it's an AMAZING one to be a member of - £0.00 a year fee, the only rules – be yourself 100% of the time, love your life, enjoy the people that are a part of it and at times, challenge yourself, do something different and do something for someone else, you might truly make their day, give it a go... what's the worst that could actually happen in the grand scheme of it all?

Don't Waste Your Life!

As I'm writing the next phase of this book, awful atrocities have been inflicting the world more and more, terror attacks just being one example. In uncertain times such as these, it's so important to realise how lucky we all are to be alive, sometimes just the fact that you're alive can be the most amazing thing of all, we only have 1 life and we really mustn't waste it. Events such as those really are sickening and can make you feel helpless, scared and worry about the future – I'm sure we've all had similar thoughts when situations have happened over the last few years. If anything, this should encourage you to live YOUR life the way YOU choose, so many people all over the world are forced against their will to live a lie, to live a certain way to protect themselves from violence or any other unimaginable horror. Most of us that live in the western world are extremely lucky, I thank the universe every day that I'm a free individual – I get to do what I want when I want. My heads not in the clouds, I realise what a luxury that is – FREEDOM and getting to be the person I choose. When you have a time when you're feeling down, have a think about people in third world countries or those caught up in conflict, I imagine you'll immediately start feeling better and the sadness will soon pass. I'm not saying that to say you can never feel down or sad, we're humans and it happens to EVERYONE, most months I'll have several times when I'm just not feeling it, or I just couldn't be bothered to do something, NOBODY is perfect... remember that, it's ok to take a breather, it's ok to re-group and take stock every once in a while.

It's what you do afterwards that really matters. What does a horse rider do if they fall off a horse? You dust yourself off, get back on the saddle and KEEP on riding, no matter how hard it gets, how bumpy the ground under your feet might feel just KEEP on going, the smooth road will soon appear and then you'll realise how truly amazing life really is. That's a pretty simple explanation of what to do when those times do appear, sometimes out of nowhere and we don't know what to do. Maybe you panic, maybe you feel like you just can't take anymore, and you want to give up trying. I've had all of those thoughts and feelings, there truly frightening and sometimes it can feel like you're down on your luck. Somehow and I honestly don't know how it happens at the time, but it usually does, you pick yourself up and keep on trekking, until the comfortable road appears, and things seem to go from bad to manageable, manageable to comfortable and then comfortable to... wow, things are going really well!

I can't give you a time scale on that though, I just can't, because it's different for everyone depending on your situation and how your life is going. BUT, with determination, the inner strength that I KNOW you possess and just a little FAITH, it will happen. It will be like all of a sudden you wake up and realise that things really are going well and its like it just all fell into place without you really thinking about it. Just remember that famous quote *"Rome wasn't built in a day"* that saying can be used for most things in life. Want a career change but realise it's going to take months or even years of training, that's fine because Rome wasn't built in a day! Or maybe you want to buy a new car and you work out its going to take 6 months to save the money to buy it, that's fine, sort out a spreadsheet and start saving, don't complain and just feel like you'll get that car with the new knowledge you now have. Another thing is to say it out loud, for example *"I will get that car" "I'm so excited to fill it with new mats and accessories"* etc. Just by saying those things and by already acting like it's in your life right now, you're halfway there! By using the Law of Attraction with the manifestation phrases and then working hard with your own determination by saving, I reckon you'll save the money in almost half the time you would have by just saving and feeling negative about the time it would have took to save in the first place. The car one is just an example and it could be something completely different, it doesn't always have to be a materialistic item, it could be a way you want to feel, a person you want to meet or the you that you want to become.

Chapter 25
We're ALL Different

The material stuff is great but it's certainly not the be all and end all. Now, I buy items because I enjoy them, not to make me feel better about myself. The latter was true a good few years back. I'd buy clothes and wear them to make myself feel better, to make me feel better about myself for a short while. Then I'd get back, put the stuff away and go back to feeling sad again. I realised that the things I was buying weren't making me happy, it was a pointless task and it just wasn't healthy. After working on personal growth and doing the meditations, healing and manifestations, I felt good no matter what I wore, no matter what condition my skin was in or any other factor, whereas before I'd have to be fully dressed up and covered in makeup before I felt good. How different things are now, it really is unreal how much I changed, I guess I had no choice, I knew there was a different version of Jack somewhere beyond the horizon, it just took me a little while to find him. Now I have, I'm never letting him go.

The amazing thing is that now I buy clothes and other items because I genuinely enjoy them, I genuinely enjoy exploring new fashion styles and dressing up. It's fun for me now and I feel good if I'm dressed up or if my hair is messy and wearing my gym wear and old dirty trainers – like I am right now as I'm typing this at home. Trust me it really is a great feeling no longer searching for perfection and trying to be "perfect" all the time – whatever that means anyway. Now, it's just about waking up and facing the day no matter what. If I want to dress up for no particular reason I WILL do, if I want to chuck on my gym gear because I couldn't be bothered to wear anything else than I WILL do. The version of Jack a few years back would have shuddered with dread if I'd had seen myself now. The difference is with the inside, how I now feel when I look at myself in that tracksuit, I feel amazing, happy and confident, no longer obsessed with pointing out flaws and taking 50 selfies to only think that they're STILL not good enough. Instead I just take a maximum of 4 or 5 now and force myself to choose 1 to upload when I do decide to do that. To begin with it felt weird but eventually it was refreshing and meant I now enjoy taking an occasional selfie.

I know many people my age in particular can relate to this and will know how incredibly hard it is to not judge ourselves. When we do judge ourselves, we realise that again, it's usually US making things so much worse for ourselves. Usually if were obsessing over an imperfection a friend or anyone we come into contact with will say they *"can't even notice it"*, because to them it just doesn't seem as bad, it's like when we look at ourselves we use a magnifying glass when looking, we making everything look and feel ten times worse, then were told that it actually isn't that bad. So take it from someone who knows, nothing is usually as bad as it first appears to be, now, go take that damn selfie!

Be Imperfectly Perfect!

Don't get me wrong, I do occasionally feel myself
looking at myself and picking out things such as a spot
on my face, but I then click back into my mode of
realising that it's honestly OK, why does that or any
other physical factor have to be such a BIG deal?! It
honestly doesn't. Let's have a think, shall we? If I have
bad hair that's just not working, will it mean I have a
shit day? Will it mean that something awful happens?
The answer is NO. We create these little stories in our
mind and think that if our skin is bad or something isn't
right then we will have a bad day, it's just not the case!
It doesn't matter what we look like, it WON'T define
how our day goes or how people view us. If it does
affect how people view you then what sort of person
does it make them? Instead, it's OUR attitude and
BELIEFS that will, the thoughts we choose to think and
the constant judgements we make about ourselves
daily. Just by having that attitude of thinking the bad
hair will ruin your day, it immediately puts you in a
negative space and frame of mind, it's almost like you
make the day bad by telling everyone you meet *"my
hair is so bad, it's really annoying me!"*. Calm down
and instead think *"eugh, my hair doesn't look great,
but it really won't affect anything I'm going to do with
my day, let's go out and get shit done!"* I've done this
so much; trust me it really works and means that you
then have this attitude of motivation and you'll find that
your day does go well and that bad hair or ungroomed
eyebrows honestly… don't matter… trust me. You'll
probably find that if you don't mention it in
conversation to the people you meet then they won't
either. Most of the time our physical appearances seem
MUCH worse to ourselves than they do to anybody

else, it's just the way we self-criticise ourselves. I'm pretty sure even drop-dead gorgeous models criticise their looks every now and then. I really hope that helps, especially people my age or even younger as I know with the likes of Instagram, reality TV and other forms of media that this feeling is only heightened more. Just remember, life is WAY too short to spend another day at war with yourself. LET GO, have FUN, be FREE… and please, stop CARING SO MUCH. Yes, care and take pride in your appearance, I do it daily, but not to the point where it's having a negative effect on your mood, your physical appearance doesn't and never will DEFINE YOUR BEAUTY, what defines your beauty is your personality, the words you say, the actions you make, not the state of your skin or body size.

Chapter 26
Inner Beauty

Beauty, what is beauty? The answer to this question will be different to everyone you ask. If you asked 10 people in a room what beauty was to them then you'd most likely get 10 different answers. To me beauty doesn't just have to be about looks, these days it can be hard for people to see that, definitely due to the rise in air brushing our photos for social media – something that I'm guilty of! I admit like most people; I like to see my photos looking blemish free and "perfect". Only yesterday I decided to take a photo and upload it to social media with ZERO adjustments, no filter, no blemish remover and ZERO skin smoothing. It felt bloody fantastic! A year or so back this is something I never would have dreamed of doing, I would have been nervous and just uncomfortable with the whole concept. Even if I don't do it again, I needed to have that "no filter" photo on my timeline, to be a constant reminder that I AM BEAUTIFUL and that I DON'T NEED to constantly edit and change things on photos. By this point I had already been practicing self-love for a year and had become pretty comfortable with myself, uploading that photo was the next step and truly showed me how far I had come.

Why don't you upload a no filter photo today... again, you'll probably find that people like and appreciate it a lot more, because we have respect for others when they are being true to themselves and giving us them, flaws and all, the flaws make us human, without them we'd almost be like perfect robots, but were not, we've lived through hardships, had ups and downs, our bodies and appearance changes as a result of going through this... so, cut yourself a bit of slack every once in a while.

Love Your Flaws!

So, why am I rabbiting on telling you about this? Because I don't believe someone's physical appearance makes them anymore beautiful then someone with a face full of acne breakouts, does that make them any less of a person? NO, of course it doesn't! Does it mean they have to cake their face in layers of makeup just to feel like they are acceptable... NO, it doesn't! If they enjoy makeup and want to use it then that's totally fine, what's not fine is using it because they genuinely feel like they have to and have no other choice. You could have someone with the face of a god and actually, their personality just isn't very nice. You could have someone with the face of a god, and they are an incredibly nice person, and the same for anyone with any physical blemish or deformity. To me, inner beauty is the thing that's truly worth its weight in gold. It took such a long time for me to say that and god knows that I know how hard it is with how we now are with the appearance obsessed society we now exist within. Be BEAUTIFUL inside and out! Compliment someone for the shear hell of it, wear ZERO makeup and rock it like a true goddess, laugh at yourself when you make mistakes and most of all, DON'T take yourself too seriously. I can't tell you how empowering it feels to sometimes not make an effort. I took that photo I mentioned, after getting back from the gym when I felt like a hot sweaty mess... better time than ever right? Even my hair was out of its usual style, I just didn't care! It felt great once I did it and the support I got really meant so much to me. I urge you to try it, even if you have a face full of what you think are "imperfections" just give it a go... I'd love to see!

Chapter 27

We're ALL in This Together

First of all, did the name of this chapter make anyone think of the song from High School? People, people, people. The types of people that you choose to surround yourself with can ultimately make a huge difference in how you live your life and succeed too. I was always one of those people that thought I'd never find true and REAL friends, I longed to find it but that negative talk and attitude was honestly getting me nowhere. Little did I know at that point what the Law of Attraction even was, I doubt I'd have listened if someone did try to explain it to me, remember when I said I used to laugh and joke at positive / inspirational quotes? Now I practically live my life by them. When I started my "journey" I remember writing this manifestation down: *"I want to find a group of real friends that accept me for who I am."* It felt empowering to write it down and had high hopes for what was to come. I remember during that initial period that I kept telling myself to not change in order to fit in with people, I've tried that before and it honestly doesn't work. I stayed me, I didn't let myself change in order to become "cool", whatever that means. It worked, tenfold!

Fast forward quite a while later and I have a really lovely circle of friends that I'd be lost without. I feel they are all there for me and I'm there for them as much as I can be, some are like family, it's a priceless feeling, especially if you've waited such a long time to finally feel like you fit in. If this type of situation rings any bells then just remember, don't panic! You might think you'll never find true friendship, you will, I'm proof of that. Now I'm accepted for who I am, accepted for the fact that I do things slightly differently and like to be over the top at times, it's just accepted. If your friends don't accept your characteristics and behaviors, then are they really friends at all? Maybe have a think about how much of a friend they are, don't give up hope because new people are just around the corner, around 7 billion in fact! Recently I was talking to a lovely friend of mine called Jen, and she was saying how one of her favorite quotes if the following *"Your vibe attracts your tribe."* It's a pretty brilliant statement to live by, it's something that absolutely works for me when I want to attract new and exciting people into my life. The vibe I put out is also attracting others towards me, my tribe if you will, realising that you have the power to create the friendships that you want is pretty powerful. If your currently thinking about your friendship groups and not liking what you're seeing then maybe have a try at switching things up a bit, your entitled to have people around you that LIFT YOU UP, that celebrate your achievements and are there to SUPPORT, you deserve nothing less so don't settle for second best.

We're ALL In this Together

You are Good Enough!

One of the worst things you can do is thinking thoughts about whether your good enough for someone, be that a boyfriend, girlfriend or just a friend, or anyone else for that matter. So many times, you hear of situations when people have breakdowns about how they feel *"not good enough"* or *"unworthy"* of someone. How dare anyone make you feel like that in the first place. YOU are absolutely 100% worthy of any person on this earth, any experience or material item, we ALL deserve to be happy, sadly this isn't always the case in certain situations. These kinds of thoughts can be truly damaging mentally and can have long lasting effects. You are good enough, you are important, and NO ONE should be allowed to make you feel anything but amazing and happy. If there not, friends and partners, maybe have a think about how you can change this, it really isn't fair if its having a negative effect on your life or mental health. Maybe you talk to them and are said to be overreacting or maybe they just can't see things from your perspective. That's ok because we are all different, we do all want different things. No one will agree with each other 100% of the time, that's just life. It will feel so empowering to make someone realise how they make you feel; it will force them to face things that maybe they're not completely comfortable with. The truth is that sometimes we do have to do things we're not comfortable with. You'll only grow as a person if you do things that make you feel uncomfortable, things that you wouldn't usually consider doing, just try it for yourself from time to time. When you do something like this you feel so fantastic once you've done it, you wonder why you worried in the first place, you realise that YOU are stronger than you realised. Stop the VICTIM mentality,

I'm saying this in the nicest way possible, I see so many people acting like the victim and feeling like they aren't good enough for someone or something, but if you have this kind of attitude and thought process your manifesting exactly what you DON'T WANT, for that very reason, because your spending so long thinking about what you don't want that's what will keep coming back and keep coming back, until you WAKE UP and realise that the person responsible for your unhappiness is YOU, because of the constant mind bullshit thoughts, because of the victim attitude. I'm saying this from a place of love and guidance, because I was the exact same and had the same attitude too, which is why I'm telling you all of this, because so many of us are thinking and living like this and wondering why we're *"so unlucky"* and we're wondering *"why can't I have something good for once"*. So, as hard as it might be I say this, try as hard as you can to start talking about WHAT YOU DO WANT and more importantly, WHAT IS GOING WELL for you right now, not the opposite which is the typical statement to make.

I don't care if the people around you think its uncool to talk or think like this, it's the crab in the bucket scenario, people won't always like it if they see you starting to change and succeed, don't give a shit what they are doing or thinking, because trust me, I know who the real winner will be in the long run. Having a positive attitude and growing mindset is GUARANTEED to get you places, you'll just need to trust me on that until you start seeing results for yourself, but you will, it might take a month or it might take a year but eventually you will absolutely see growth from wherever you direct the effort and energy to, be that career, personal growth, your relationships, finances, anything, just DON'GIVE UP!

Chapter 28

Each Day Is a Gift

Many of us probably don't realise this, but EVERY single day on planet earth is a gift. Some of us wake up each morning like we're taking the day for granted, constantly moaning about early mornings or the train being delayed… I'm guilty of this one sometimes I really can't lie. But just think for one minute, what if we didn't have a day, then you'd really realise how incredibly lucky YOU are. In the UK winter especially, we can all get into a bit of a head fog, days merge into weeks with us just getting through them, existing and not really enjoying life, such a shame, and such a waste. I totally appreciate that when the weather is crap and the mornings are dark that it can be hard to paint on a smile, just remember our mantra…. Nothing is forever. Soon the lighter mornings and seasons to follow will be upon you. In times like this it's important to be thankful for the little things.

When you've worked with the homeless, I think it changes how you view things. I've previously volunteered at homelessness charities and served meals to the many people, sometimes 100's, that visit daily. It's all too easy to take for granted that hot meal on a cold night, that hot bath and warm bed you have. Yes, these things do matter, they may seem an "essential" to your everyday life, but to someone sleeping rough on the streets this would feel like winning the lottery, see how we all have different priorities?

Giving Back is Food for the Soul!

The next exercise I want you to consider is to take up some sort of volunteering, it doesn't have to be every week or even every month, just whenever you see yourself with some free time and want to do something that will truly make a difference, I know this can vary with every person and how busy your life is.

You could do anything, volunteer to deliver hot meals to the elderly in your local area, have you got a car and an afternoon to spare? Then you're good to go. You could visit local hospitals and volunteer there; they are ALWAYS in need and would be happy for the help. You could volunteer as a staff member at your nearest weekly Brownies or Scouts club, it doesn't have to be working with vulnerable groups of people if you don't feel comfortable with that. The very best thing about volunteering anywhere is that PRICELESS feeling you get when you've done it. It could even be working an afternoon at your local charity shop or foodbank. You feel like you've made a real difference, a difference is a difference no matter how small. You could give blood; this is something I started doing not long back because I wanted to give something other than money. Being a student extra finances isn't something I have a lot of currently, so I wanted to come up with a way I could strongly benefit people instead of just a donation, that's how I got into blood donating, it costs me no actual money, just a small portion of time once every 3 months, it's all about finding a way, no matter how small, to give back and make a positive difference, it doesn't matter the size of your contribution, just having good intent to begin with is enough. So, how are you planning on giving back?

Chapter 29

Do Something Different

I think many more of us would do things like
volunteering or anything else if it wasn't for our prior
thoughts and feelings about doing it. Many worry about
the time needed, will they like it, will they be able to
handle it? As I've previously mentioned, many of us
won't do things in life because we're either scared or
feel uncomfortable, usually because it's something
different or not the norm. Life is so short that I tell you
this… DO IT! Can you ever recall a time in your life
when you said no to something just because you hadn't
done it before or felt scared or any other similar
emotion? I can put my hand up to this. We make
excuses up in our mind about why we shouldn't do it,
it's almost like our very own mind is trying to convince
us to not do it before we've even given it a try. The new
mantra I live by is that I'll try anything once, then if I
don't like it, I don't have to do it again… Simple.

So, whatever it is, give it a try and then if you can still say that you feel uncomfortable and that you're honestly not enjoying it then you don't have to do it again. No one should ever make you do something you don't want to do, maybe if we were all told this from the start we wouldn't get so stressed out and anxious about doing something for the first time, we'd feel slightly better after being told we wouldn't have to do it again if we didn't want to. Sometimes though we have to do things in life that we really don't want to do, I can't give you a straightforward answer as to why this is, I'm still trying to figure that out myself. I have had those moments though where I've looked back on experiences and realised years later why I had to go through them, usually to get to the good stuff. Try telling me that in the moment and I'd most likely say it was a load of crap, these days whenever I'm going through a challenging situation, I always remember how STRONG I am, how DETERMINED I am and that as always, it's not FOREVER.

So, whatever situation you find yourself in at this very moment, be that a good or bad one, just remember, it will change, it will alter, it won't go on forever. If things are going well then maybe consider this from a place of feeling GRATITUDE, because it might not last forever I urge you to enjoy every single second of whatever it might be, don't waste the time and don't let the opportunity pass you by without giving 110% effort to whatever it is. Likewise, if you're not enjoying your current situation instead of having the victim mentality of feeling sorry for yourself and constantly complaining let this feeling give you fuel to DEMAND MORE, because everyone deserves more, everyone deserves to do something that does make them want to get out of bed in the morning and absolutely SMASH IT. Make your vision board, visualize once, twice or five times a day if you need to, anything to get you through the dark tunnel of whatever is happening now, it doesn't have to define you and it certainly doesn't need to determine your happiness... not if you let it.

Chapter 30

Make the Impossible Possible

Sometimes you think that something is "impossible", even when you know that really, it isn't, it's just that we're either too scared or afraid of what will happen when we do it… maybe people will laugh, maybe we will be judged, maybe people won't care… all negative feelings that I could list forever. A common example I want to refer to is public speaking, something I used to absolutely hate with a passion. For me speaking in front of anyone was always a fear, just putting myself out there and being in front of others speaking filled me with dread and a ton of anxiety. I can remember so much years ago in school and college, where we were told we'd be presenting in front of the class, usually in a group, not that this made me feel any better about the situation. It's weird that when you logically think about it, it's just doing the thing we can all do… to talk! Other fears like spiders you'd presume would be feared more, but no, public speaking is one of the biggest fears most humans have.

Not so long ago I challenged this and had to personally think why I was afraid of such a simple action. For me I realised it was because I have a slightly higher voice than the average male, so for some weird reason I let this make me hate the idea of public speaking, but does anyone give a shit? In my head I worked myself up so much and basically created some mind bullshit, something that didn't really matter, yes, I have a slightly higher voice, is it the highest voice ever, is it strange…. NO, so why does it even matter? Well clearly, it doesn't. Not so long ago I had to do a presentation on a whole new level, it was for my university module where I had to present at a PR conference in a packed room filled with professionals, totally different to the small presentations I used to get beyond scared about. At this point though I'd been practicing mindfulness and using the Law of Attraction for 2 years which meant I was in a totally different mindset to what I was a few years previously. This time I wasn't scared one bit, but I was still nervous due to the fact that this was the first presentation I'd done in years.

This time I had a plan, I spent every night for 2 weeks watching videos on YouTube about how to confidently do public speaking, I studied them and applied them to my own presentation. Along with this I practiced, several times and knew that finally I could do it, I'm proud of my voice now, proud of myself and knew I was ready. The week of the presentation I came down with the worst virus, it wasn't good and meant for the days leading up I couldn't rehearse like I wanted to. The day of the presentation came, I had a pretty groggy voice from the virus and cough but as ever determined as I now am I absolutely smashed it, I have no idea how. My group at the conference presenting was in the biggest room, imagine a huge room with rows and rows of chairs on either side, and little old me in the middle presenting. Another problem I always had was giving eye contact, usually I'd stare down at notes and rarely look up, I was just too nervous. This time I rarely even looked at the notes, instead I asked the audience questions and actually engaged... it's amazing how everything changes when you ENGAGE with others, just talk to them, have a conversation and stop caring about what others think, you're never going to please everybody. Considering how ill I felt leading up it was hand on heart the best presentation I have ever done in 2 years, I spoke and looked all around the room, giving eye contact to everyone and didn't really bother looking down at my notes for long at all. After finishing I can't describe the feeling of elation, it's pretty amazing when you FINALLY achieve something you've wanted to do for so long. I can't tell you how many times years ago I'd finish a presentation and feel deflated, knowing that I could do better, this time was the complete opposite. What feels big to one person doesn't to everyone, for you this might be an everyday thing and not be a big deal, but to me it was and felt bloody fantastic. This was yet again proof that you really CAN do whatever you put your mind to, just remember, it isn't a race. So, what is it that scares you that you want to tackle? Maybe you want to play a new sport, or travel somewhere new, or learn a new language... anything that has previously made you feel nervous and apprehensive, it could be anything. Why not stop reading now and make a plan on how you're going to do it, remember, if you don't at least try, you'll never know the end outcome, you'll never get to see how truly amazing it could be, or maybe it will go wrong and you'll learn it isn't for you, who cares, just GIVE IT A GO!

Chapter 31

Life Situations

Instead of constantly writing this book you're reading right now, I've had large gaps, sometimes of 5-6 months. This isn't because I've had writers block or haven't had the inspiration, it's been on purpose. As cliché as it sounds life is honestly a journey, so for me I've put the book down and just experienced life in between, picking up more tips and opinions along the way. I can honestly say that when this book finally reaches you I'll probably have lots of new advice to pass on, I started writing this book when I was 19 and now I'm 21 so I've definitely got much more of life to experience, but I've certainly grown a lot in the last 2 years, I can't imagine my life without the Law of Attraction and having the tools that I now use daily in order to stay in a healthy mind and wellbeing. I even joke now that I'm a ¾ glass full person, I always look on the positive side, even when sometimes, it may be hard to find one. Take death for instance.

When my Nan died in 2010 it honestly felt like the end of the world, like nothing would be the same again, the second statement was certainly right. Fast forward 8 years and I can still say that most days I will think about my Nan, even if it's just a passing thought. For me I was beyond close with her, she was like a second Mom and her and my Grandpa would often look after me and my Sister during the week and at school holidays when my Mom would be working all the hours god sent to give me and my Sister a good life. She died at 78 which isn't the best age, but she was out of pain, and that gave us comfort. For me dealing with that tested me in every single way, I didn't even look at photos of her for a few years after, just doing it would mean I'd burst into tears. Because I felt so young when she died, I often thought for years, and still do, if she'd be proud of me, be proud of the choices I've made so far in life and accept my sexuality…. I know she would, but you always want that reassurance from those closest to you. 8 years later though I choose to remember her in the best way, from her amazing fashion sense to her funny wit, she was honestly an amazing women and was an amazing Mom herself and grandparent to me and my Sister.

Not everyone chooses to believe that people that have passed on can be contacted, but since then I've seen my Nan several times, too many to remember because obviously I haven't physically seen her body in a human form, but I've felt her several times, even in our living room once, it was clear to me that for just a few minutes she was watching me and what I was doing, I could immediately tell that she had left when she did. The point I'm trying to get across to you here, because I certainly don't know lots, is that IT WILL GET BETTER, you just have to trust that. It feels like it's the end of the world, it feels like it will never get better, like you'll feel sad forever. It's almost like that one day you just wake up and things don't feel so bad as the previous day, and so on and so on. There will always be days that you miss them more, such as Birthdays and other occasions but just remember, if you really want to see them again, you can, if you really want to send them love, you can. It does get better, little by little, day by day. They say that time is the best healer, it's a statement I do believe to be true for many different circumstances, such as falling out with friends, losing a loved one, experiencing something that has a deep effect on you mentally or physically, sometimes time and time alone is the biggest thing, so just wait, because eventually and even if it feels like it won't, it will get better.

<u>Don't Give Up!</u>

I mentioned earlier on about making friends and that feeling like you'll never find them. I'm at the point now where keeping my circle small is honestly all I want. Some people want the biggest group of friends, probably not caring too much about the quality of those friends, their morals and what they believe in. Quality over quantity is definitely the motto I live by now, in most areas of my life, not just friends. I have such an amazing circle now, from all different areas of the UK too. I have friends in uni who I see regularly, but on the other hand I have friends who live in all different areas of the country, north and south, who I speak to everyday in some cases. For me I think the problem is that I used to limit myself, and the way I'd make friends. Some people believe that you can only make friends face to face who are in your immediate life, such as work colleagues, people on your college course or neighborhood etc. What I've learnt is that I can make friends with whoever, I even have a friend who lives in Hawaii. It took a long while for me to find people that I had a connection with, some of these friends don't have the same interests as me though, we just get on well and they have that energy I'm looking for in a person.

So, remember, don't be afraid to be picky, you don't want your time wasted so don't be afraid to make friends via social media either. I've made many good friends just through Instagram, we used to like each other's posts and then you get chatting and I've met up with several of them and now call them friends. It's strange because before meeting up you feel like you already know the person, you speak with them and see their life through the content they decide to post, so actually, for me it was less daunting meeting up with them then being at my first day of uni and meeting new people. Let's face it, by then the person already knows you're a little crazy and accepts it, and if you say you're not crazy then you're lying... EVERYONE has a few ounces of crazy in them, it's good for you. I wish I had been given this advice a few years back, because I couldn't find friends close to me in location I thought that was it, no other option, but now I sometimes speak to my friends online more than my uni friends who I've had loads of memories with, but that's fine because now I have an awesome selection of friends I can chat to for a variety of things. For me I'm so simple now when it comes to making friends, I look for 2 things: that they have positive energy, not meaning they need to be happy everyday but just to have that good "feeling" about them, and secondly that they can SUPPORT ME in what I DO, and I can SUPPORT THEM in what THEY DO... it's that simple! Then with this that's a solid support to any relationship in general, then everything else will come with time, every good friendship needs time to build, to get to know someone and then when you know them fully you can unleash the true weirdness you possess.

Chapter 32
Sometimes we Fall

I want to talk about something I experienced recently, that totally challenged me and eventually, helped me grow a great deal. I was visiting the annual Gay Pride festival in my city, an amazing day having fun, listening to music and just being surrounded by fun and VERY colourful people, they have them all over the world and it's such a beautiful celebration for diversity in all its forms. That's actually very appropriate, because I want to talk about being yourself... again! I repeat myself on certain points for a reason, I want you to know it so much it will become ingrained in you and become second nature. The afternoon before going I was in the city preparing stuff I needed to do and just got this overwhelming sense of fear and nerves, I felt scared to go, scared in general, it was the worst kind of crippling anxiety, something I've experienced at different times throughout my life. Bear in mind I classed myself as a fairly confident person at this point, I had no problem with expressing myself and had even visited Pride the year before. My outfit was very colourful and involved this amazing jacket with glitter and colourful thread tassels up the arms, along with a sequin bag round my waist. I suppose for me being gay has always meant I've had fears in the back of my head, fear of what others will think, how they will react etc.

When I analysed the fear I was feeling on that Friday afternoon I could see that, subconsciously, I had been thinking about it for a long time before the event. For me this made me realise that we will ALWAYS have these doubts and negative thoughts, but it's how we deal with them that really counts. I still get negative and limiting thoughts now, even after the different practices I have, it's just like the volume of them has been turned down a lot more than it ever was before. To cut a long story short that day was the best day, ten times better than Pride the year before and I loved every single second, wearing my outfit with PRIDE no matter where I went. Did anything happen... of course not. This did teach me a very valuable lesson though. In that situation on the Friday afternoon when I truly panicked, and my breathing got very heavy, and I felt like I was having the onset of an anxiety attack, I had two choices. I could have believed those thoughts; I could have decided in that moment to change my outfit to something more "conservative" or even to decide to not go at all. Or, I could choose to totally ignore those thoughts, to not fight them and instead let them wash over my body like a giant wave, and then after my breathing had got back to normal, when I was in a normative state, to then decide what to do.

Thankfully I was at a good level of mindfulness after doing it for 2 years and decided to totally ignore them and this situation made me even more determined to have the most amazing day, and that's exactly what I did. What happened that day in late May 2018 made me realise that actually, we are ALWAYS learning, we will ALWAYS face obstacles, of some kind, but it's how we link them in our head, do we link them to negativity and make ourselves feel depressed and miserable, or instead, do we link them to us having to learn a life lesson, knowing that it will make us stronger and even more determined to be our true selves in the process? I know which one I'll pick, EVERY SINGLE TIME.

You could decide to link this situation to pain, I could have even said that this proved I was weak, and that the last 2 years had been for nothing, the old me would certainly have said this, I was forever thinking negative and extremely destructive thoughts. I don't think many people realise how destructive their actual THOUGHTS are, they might think that just because they haven't said it out loud and are only thinking it then it isn't making any kind of problem… sadly this couldn't be any further from the truth.

The best way to do this is to do the following: tomorrow morning wake up and mentally say that TODAY IS GOING TO BE A GREAT DAY, if you want you can say it out loud too. Wait and see what happens, because I can absolutely guarantee that at least 1 good thing will happen, if you look for the positive, you'll find it, and this is something I will never stop saying. Why is it that people can easily find the negative in something, are so quick to criticize, so quick to judge or pick the bad points out of a person or object, then the positive, or lack of positives ALWAYS seems to come second? Instead we need to start doing the opposite, list all the positives first, speaking about what you do like, what you do enjoy about a person. A saying I used to be told when I was a little boy was if you don't have anything positive to say don't say ANYTHING at all. I think many of us need to start practicing this in our own lives. Because yes, these kind of comments and thoughts are damaging and may upset those we say them to, but you have no idea how damaging and destructive they are to you and your life. The next time you go to say something negative, just think to yourself first, do I really want to say this, do I really want to go there? Again, YOUR THOUGHTS are YOUR CHOICE, I will say it again so it sticks, no one forces you to think a negative thought, yes, things might not be going well for you currently, but just dig as deep as you can to find the things you are grateful for in your life, everyone can write a list of them.

Stop Defining!

This experience from gay Pride has to bring me onto how we as humans let things define us. So many things can define us, if we let them, such as sexuality, race, gender, our family, our upbringing, being in an abusive relationship, experiencing death and utter heartbreak… the list is endless. Sadly, but truly I can say that I let being gay define me for a long time until I decided it no longer could, and ever since it's been pretty incredible, just being myself and being the real me without having to pretend to be something I wasn't. For me it's like I woke up one day and said enough is enough, I can't do this any longer. Now I don't see my sexuality as a defining factor, like it's a tiny piece of Jack Walton. Yes, I like the same sex, but it doesn't change how I think, what I like or what I do. If I like something I like it and if I want to do something I'll do it, no matter what it is, if I'm happy that's all that matters… how amazing is that mindset, this is how I've been thinking for the last 2 years and has meant I've had some truly amazing experiences, again, no one forced me to start thinking differently, I just knew I demanded more out of life and out of my self, so I knew I had to make some big changes in order to achieve what I wanted.

It's harder to do something you fear then it is to carry on keeping it a secret, or carrying on faking something, because the very thought of deciding to change and leave that comfort zone you're in, is so scary. I could have easily carried on being a fake version of myself, but I know all these experiences and opportunities I've manifested for myself in the last 2 years just wouldn't be my reality. Does this sound like something you're experiencing, because I can tell you the mental effort it takes to change is immense, sometimes it feels like it isn't worth the risk, again you can doubt yourself ALL DAY LONG but if you don't give something a go you'll never know. There are so many examples of things that define us, but I just want to tell you about my own personal ones, in the hope that just one person reading this will be able to relate and decide that today is the LAST DAY they are going to let whatever it may be, define them as an individual, as a human being and basically RULE THEIR LIFE.

The only person that should be ruling your life is YOU, so why do we let ourselves be defined by our past, by our mistakes. We ALL make mistakes, nobody is "perfect", we're all just learning. A second example for me would be the poor mental health I had for 3 years, PTSD, anxiety and social anxiety. I was at the darkest points when several nights I'd say to myself in my head, and out loud, that I didn't want to wake up the next morning, I just didn't want to bother. Years later I could have let that define me. Instead I wear it as a positive, I tell people how much I suffered and how I came through the tunnel at the end, that's the point I SURVIVED, I'm a SURVIVER. If you can sit here now and say that you survived whatever it is that happened to you, then that's already a huge achievement, we don't celebrate our achievements enough. Everyone reading this can automatically say that as if you hadn't had survived… you wouldn't be reading this right now! Since then I've had the courage to talk on camera for the BBC about my past experiences, raise money for a mental health charity, I speak on Instagram about how I dealt with it and the best thing I did recently was speak in front of an audience, including my family, about my mental health, what happened, and how eventually, I did find the light again. I used to think that there was no light at the end of the tunnel, but there is, trust me. Just remember, it does and WILL get better, and NOTHING is forever, I PROMISE you'll find that LIGHT AGAIN.

Turning that example around I could have easily let those past experiences define me, feeling embarrassed whenever the topic is bought up, feel nervous to open up to friends, and in general let it hold me back in everyday life, but I DIDN'T, I refused to let it define me. I'm not trying to glamorize mental health here, it did have a hugely poor impact on my life and wellbeing, I did wake up each day with dread, I felt tired all of the time and had no spark for anything if I'm honest, I'm not glossing over this either, I could go into much more detail about my own mental health but for me I'd rather shine the spotlight on my recovery instead and how I DID GET BETTER, because trust me, I never thought I would, ever, I had zero hope of things changing. I'm writing this book because I want to reach those who may be in a similar situation to this, who might be totally helpless and feel like giving up, but then, things do begin to change when you sometimes least expect it, so keep on going, I BELIEVE in YOU!

Chapter 33

Just do You

Ever heard that saying, the grass may be greener on the other side? I want to talk about how so often we spend time focusing on everyone else's lush green grass that we forget to focus on our own so ours starts to die and turns brown... nobody wants brown grass! I used to do this so much, so interested on what other people are doing with their lives and then neglecting mine as a result. This is something I mentioned earlier on but something I want to touch on again. For me I have some amazing friends and family in my life that I truly feel blessed to have, I love them all dearly and love seeing their achievements and what they are getting up to. Doing that is just being supportive and is totally fine, but what's not fine is when you're focusing on others so much you don't focus on yourself. I'm at a stage in life now where sadly I'm too busy tending to my own grass to notice how green anyone else's is, and this is the same attitude you NEED to adopt if you want to be truly successful in life, remember, you're in the driver's seat of your own life, not the passenger looking on.

You need to adopt this attitude because when you do, you realise that actually, that's what the majority of people are doing. For me I focus on myself but still have time for others, it's not being selfish, it's just using your time wisely. Instead of looking at where your friends are going you need to plan on where YOU'RE going instead. Instead of looking at people in the gym and how they work out, yes you can look to take some inspiration from them, but then decide how YOU want to exercise and what you need to do in order to achieve what you want… not just in the gym but for all areas of your life. For so long I can honestly say I didn't give my own life much attention, instead I'd care what others were doing, where they were going, what they were achieving, this meant I got in a totally negative pattern of basically self-neglection, like I just didn't care… looking back now this was most likely because I just didn't feel much self-worth, I honestly didn't and I'm saying this because I want to be 100% honest and tell you how I did totally change my life in around 2 years. It really was like a before and after and proved to me that if someone can change their thinking patterns which leads to more achievement, fulfilment and happiness, how amazing is that? Everyone needs to be firmly in the driver's seat of their life, are you?

Do it Today, Not Tomorrow!

I'm going to use the gym as another example for something I want to talk about, when we put things off to do tomorrow which could just be done today if we really wanted to. Not so long ago I joined the gym again, I have periods of time usually in the winter when I'll stop going because life just gets in the way. Lately I went back and that first day going was beyond hard, it feels such an effort and the fact it was pouring with rain that morning certainly didn't help. In that moment I could have easily decided the weather was too bad and to instead, go the following morning, trust me I was beyond tempted to. But then the next morning could have come and then I could have EASILY made a second excuse… you can see how this pattern is forming. You might have a similar situation in your life, something that you know you need to start or do, but instead you say you'll do it the next day or the day after that etc. It's so easy to do this but instead I went for it, I went and had the most amazing gym session and have been loving it ever since, this could have been a very different set of circumstances if instead I decided to let the weather beat me and not go.

If you're wanting to stop smoking for example, as humans, we are great at doing one thing in particular… MAKING EXCUSES! Making excuses by saying you won't stop smoking until your stressful life gets better, or whatever situation improves… but isn't that just making an excuse to carry on smoking? If there was an Olympics for it I'm sure most of us would win gold, it's so easy to blame something, someone else, but rarely do we put the blame or responsibility on ourselves. I wonder why that is then, because we don't want to feel we are in charge of our OWN lives, because that's too scary, that's too of a heavy burden for us to even think about, even for a second. Instead we're more than happy to put the blame on others. Many think it's scary to actually believe we are in control of our own lives because many feel controlled by others and just follow the crowd… I definitely don't do this; I do the opposite. Every single day I realise that I'm in control of my life, I can do whatever I want, go wherever I want, and most importantly BE WHOEVER I want. Remember, the only person who is getting in the way of your happiness is YOU. YOU are responsible for yourself, so start living your life with this attitude. Wake up every day and feel that sense of being in charge, in charge of your brain, your thoughts, how those thoughts then control you, or don't etc. The only person who is standing in your way is YOU, the negative and limiting thoughts telling you that you can't achieve something, telling you that you're not good enough, it's all in your OWN MIND, we're literally sabotaging things for ourselves and from doing it for such a long time and now looking back, I can certainly see how easy it is to start believing your own self-deprecating bullshit.

Chapter 34

Rule your Own Mind

We can sometimes have so many negative thoughts about something those very thoughts can then stop you doing whatever it might be, like going to a job interview as a generic example. If someone really wanted to, they could make sure they didn't attend the job interview they have been offered, they could work themselves up so much in the days leading up to the interview, by thinking lots of negative thoughts about the person not liking them, or them getting all the questions wrong etc. Let's be honest we can all agree how easy it is to think negative thoughts, so why don't many realise how EASY it is to think positive thoughts too, because it is. You may not believe it right now, but you could easily make yourself not go to that interview and you can easily say to me that I don't have a clue what I'm talking about, and how dare I suggest that you have basically self-sabotaged yourself. This, however, can be the case in many situations. Some people are so used to putting themselves down, so used to being negative that they basically sabotage situations… all by themselves, how sad is that?!

So, stop feeling sorry for yourself because I'm not here to give out bags of sympathy, I'm here to try and get you to understand and realise that you can just as easily fill your mind with positive thoughts, think that, yes, the interview will go well, it WILL be a good experience. I bet if you do this and think that positively before the interview it will go well, and even if it doesn't you won't feel as bad as you would have if you were to have filled your mind with negative thoughts instead…. It's not rocket science in reality, it's so easy but for years I didn't realise any of this so I'm only here to spread this message to others, if you agree with me or not that's totally fine, all I know is what has worked for me and what hopefully, will work for you.

Going back to the quote I gave you about the grass being greener, the truth is that yes, it might be. You might be a single parent living in a council house looking at the grass of some highly successful family. The thing you need to do instead of constantly looking at them and thinking how "lucky" they are, you instead need to think, ok, this might not be me right now but it's not totally impossible, because the truth is, it isn't, NOTHING IS IMPOSSIBLE! If more people believed this the world would be so much more of a beautiful place, people just supporting each other and being happy when someone is successful, instead of being petty and jealous, which again, WON'T GET YOU ANYWHERE... so stop. That single parent example may even be true for someone reading this book, just keep focusing on your own grass and focusing on what you want to do, maybe take up a new hobby, apply for a new job, visit a new place.

I honestly don't give a shit who you are, and I mean this in the nicest possible way, because no matter who you are this won't stop you achieving whatever you put your mind too, it honestly won't. If you have the following characteristics, I promise you it will pay off in the long run: **DEDICATION**, being dedicated to whatever it is you're doing, like doing a workout at the gym. **DETERMINATION**, feeling determined and being honest about the fact that yes, it might take a while, but you're so determined you won't take no for an answer, it's not even in your vocabulary. Another important word is **PERSISTANCE,** this can be a good thing and sometimes a bad thing and it's something I've always stuck too, being persistent means that even in despite of difficulty or knock backs (which I've had and do have plenty of!), you won't stop until you've achieved what you want, even when times get tough and no matter how many times you fall off the horse, you'll get up, pat yourself off and carry on riding. Just by applying **DEDICATION, DETERMINATION & PERSISTANCE** to your life I can absolutely promise you you'll see progress like you've never seen before, things are guaranteed to happen quicker… I'm not saying it's going to be easy because the best things usually aren't but, are ALWAYS worth waiting for!

Chapter 35

Focus on what You WANT

I mentioned earlier about how we can sometimes self-sabotage situations for ourselves. I don't think people realise, because if they truly did, they certainly wouldn't say and think the things they do, usually on a daily basis because for them it's just second nature and don't even consider it to be negative or damaging... but it honestly is. It's been proven in the past and I've also had personal experience of how we as humans, can make ourselves poorly or feel better just by the thoughts we think. If you're dreading an upcoming day and want to wake up feeling sick so you can't go, trust me, that will happen, we really DO have the power to make ourselves ill without even catching a virus or bug... it's all in the mind. I am talking from personal experience here.

Years ago, when I had things coming up that were pretty big days, maybe I was visiting someone, I'd repeatedly think in the days leading up to it that I hoped I wouldn't be poorly, I hoped I'd be ok. Can you guess what happened, usually I would wake up and feel poorly, although I wasn't actually asking for this to happen at all, quite the opposite. Going back to the Law of Attraction, the factors and details we focus on will happen, because the universe doesn't here a positive or negative thought, they are all just thoughts so by me saying *"I hope I'm not poorly"*, I then woke up poorly because the universe translated that into focusing on the poorly element. You may be able to recognise what I'm trying to get at here. A lot of the time it seems to be natural to focus on what we don't want, but instead we should be focusing on what WE DO WANT and not even thinking about the stuff we don't want. I can guarantee if you are always focusing on the things you don't want then you'll carry on finding that stuff more and more. Instead you need to think about what's not going well right now and then decide what you want to change and what you do want, then focus mentally on the solution constantly, not the negative elements. That's the level of power our mind has.

Let me give you an example. If you want to manifest more money into your life than most people will focus on how little money they have and that they wish they would have more money, but in the back of our minds we still focus on the frustration and fear of not having money, of not being able to go on holiday or do some home repairs etc. Instead of doing this which I know is easier said than done, instead we need to focus on asking for more money, for more financial security, leave out the negatives, leave out the frustration of not having enough money, because I can guarantee you if instead you decide to focus on wanting more money and not focusing on NOT having enough money, you will see it come into your life much quicker… give it a go! The same goes for relationships too, if you are someone who tends to see the worst in others and pick out all the bad parts in your partner then what really is the point? Instead you should be trying your absolute best to pick out all the GOOD points, the small details that seem to be outshone by the criticism we give. It's the same if you're currently looking to attract a partner into your life, instead of listing down everything you don't want, such as, you don't want them to be a dishonest person, instead write a list down of what you DO WANT, so you might want them to be honest, you might want them to have good aspirations, whatever situation the same theory can be applied… go out looking for what you do want, instead of focusing on what you don't want or the lack of something, focus on the opposite and you're sure to see real results a lot quicker.

Chapter 36

Take a Break

One thing I'm always learning is that sometimes we just need to take a step back, we just need to take a breath and take time to relax. I mentioned earlier on how important self-care is and this is no different. Not so long back I was in a situation where I thought at the time I was having negative feelings and confusion but then after this I had to travel away for 4 days and once I returned I realised I wasn't going crazy, I wasn't in fact feeling how I thought I did only 5 days prior to this. This example showed me that sometimes taking a break with some different scenery can totally give you a new perspective on things, for me it showed me what really mattered in my life and what really mattered to me. I wasn't spending the time relaxing, quite the opposite in fact I was actually working on a summer school looking after 15-year old's, but having a distraction almost gave me somewhat of a mental reset and I got back with a totally new attitude and felt beyond refreshed. I totally get that we can't always leave and go off somewhere, finances could be an issue or not being able to take time off work, but having time off is ok, taking time for yourself is absolutely CRUCIAL to live a healthy life and to have a good overall wellbeing. For me I do several things that give me a mental refresh, things you know already as I've mentioned them quite a few times already throughout.

First is the simplest one, meditation. I usually do this most days, if I'm super busy there's a meditation app I use called Omvana which I'm totally recommending to you as a great starting point, especially if you're new to the concept, along with Head Space, which is absolutely amazing and perfect for beginners. Sometimes I'll do a 2 minute one which just gives me that clarity I need to refresh quickly. On the app there are many sections which contain a whole variety of meditations which can work on different things, such as helping anxiety, depression, phobias etc. The next thing I do, something that I've done recently is to limit my time on social media or even have a total detox. Let's use the last example of when I taught at a summer school. During this time the days were so busy I just didn't have the time to endlessly scroll through my social media platforms which admittedly, I sometimes do (a lot!). Don't get me wrong, I don't see social media as a total negative, I enjoy getting inspiration from others and following my favorite celebrities, but sometimes it can become obsessive and take up more of our time than we realise, let's use going to the gym as my most recent example. When I'm at the gym I usually take my phone to use between working out when I want a rest, well recently I decided to not take my phone and the amount of extra work I did was pretty amazing, I got more of my working out done in much less time, I guess I didn't realise just how much I was stopping to check my social media in between exercising.

So, back to summer school. Because of all the responsibilities I had I was only going on social media twice daily, and not for very long at that. I would check in the morning when I woke up and then once at night, I ended up loving this experience because I was living in the moment and being more present, something we all need to do more of sometimes. Did I miss out on anything, no, did I suffer as a result, no, did I survive… ABSOLUTELY! As a result of this experience and realising that actually, I don't need to be on social media so much, I now check it much less and for the first time I'd definitely say I'm aware of when I've been on it a little too long. So, my mission to you, if you choose to accept it, is to limit your social media use, I want you to check it twice daily, and nothing more! Once in the morning check your profiles, then log out of them, this way it saves getting notifications which you'll be tempted to check, then once in the evening, then again, log back out… try doing this for as long as you think you can manage it, maybe a weekend as a good starting point. I've heard countless stories and there are also some books which talk about the fact we're addicted to our phones, which I suppose in some cases is true. I try as much as possible to use mine for positive, use it for good, so for me a total detox isn't really needed but just being aware of your usage and making sure going on your phone isn't meaning you're missing out on the real world is certainly important!

What next, well, seeing things from a different perspective is also important in any situation, there is ALWAYS more than one way of looking at something. When things are negative or not going our way it's so easy to only see things from one side, in the fog of confusion we don't even see the multiple other sides and options. When I have something playing on my mind or something I'm trying to work through I do something pretty simple, but it can be very effective.... MOVE! Moving out of your everyday environment can make a real difference, leave your home and go out somewhere, anywhere. Just changing where you are and having a different space to think can definitely help you see things from a different perspective. If the weather is alright the very best place you should be is outdoors, if that means going to your local park and sitting down for 3 hours until you're feeling better or have a way forward then so be it, whatever it takes for you to see that most likely, things AREN'T as bad as you realise, things CAN and WILL get better.

Taking that break almost made me realise I could cope with many different conditions, it's amazing what we can do when we have to. I had to adapt to a new routine and do things differently, it made me realise just how much Jack can cope with. When we're wrapped up in our busy everyday routines we most likely do the same things at the same times each day, I know most weekdays with being in uni that I do, this can become comfortable and we don't realise that we could be doing so much more if we really pushed ourselves, like exercising for example! Being at the gym lately and going on the rowing machine is always a challenge, usually it gets to only 2 minutes and I want to stop, I feel like I've had enough, and sometimes I could definitely stop, but instead I push myself for 10 minutes, because Jack is capable of doing 30 minutes if he wants to, it's all about pushing yourself for more, pushing yourself for BETTER. I'm not telling you to make yourself sick by doing too much, I'm just saying that there's so much going on in everybody's lives and we're all busy doing our own thing but just realise how much you're capable of and how much we CAN manage if we're forced to. Why not exit your own comfort zone for a bit and do something you've always wanted to, but been too scared of?

How we Label Situations

Another thing I'm learning is that sometimes it takes an awful situation for a positive to come as a result. Let me ask you a question, has anything what you perceive as negative ever happened to you and then later, maybe weeks, months or years, you realise it happened for a reason, you realise that actually, it turned out to be a blessing in disguise? Several times in my life negative experiences have taken place but then years later I can honestly say that they've made me the person I am today, they've made me strong and more resilient, and best of all, more determined than ever to be my very best self, to smash my goals, to travel to new places and live the life that I'm creating, no one else, just me. This will be different for each person, but it's how you view these experiences that matters.

I'll give you one of my examples and show you how it's easy to look at things from both sides, sadly most of the time we seem to only view things from the negative, therefore we label those experiences negative and therefore they won't help us grow, instead many may think these experiences have made them ill or made them hate the world. At the age of 6 my parents split up which totally devastated me, I was so young and didn't really understand what was happening, all I knew is that my Dad was no longer living at the family home with us. As I got older for years, I viewed this as negative, I would constantly say how hard it made things and how much we struggled in the years after. 2 years ago, through my mindfulness and more recently through reading the most amazing book which I'm totally recommend you buy and read after this one, it's called Awaken The Giant Within by Tony Robbins and has honestly taught me so much, it speaks lots about our references in life and how we label an experience as negative. To cut a long story short I had to tackle the key "negative" experiences in my life and try and ask myself why I labelled them and thought of them as this, could I ever possibly see them as positive, I definitely couldn't ever imagine seeing some of the experiences on my list as positive…

But, after a bit of soul searching and thinking I do now see this experience, not totally as positive, but no longer negative... it's an experience that has SHAPED me, see what I did there, I'm changing the language I use towards this experience, It's no longer negative. Because of this experience I had the most amazing childhood with my Mom and Sister, I got to express myself 100% and be my true self, I could go on by giving you the positives that did eventually, end up coming out of that experience, sometimes it just takes a while for you to see and realise them, trust me. So, the point I'm making here is to stop labelling things as negative and acting like everything is the end of the world, because it isn't. I changed the language I used, I'm not lying and saying it was totally positive because it wasn't, yes there were hard times, but it's made me the Jack I am right now and I'm ok with that, release it because once you do you can fully start to work on yourself.

Stop Looking Back!

Another thing I see so much, and I've certainly been guilty of in the past and is something I mentioned previously but mentioning again, is how we look back at what we may perceive to be "negative" situations and constantly feel that regret and hurt, but why do we do this when we CAN'T CHANGE THE PAST? It doesn't matter how upset you feel, how much you beat yourself or others up or how much you regret it, you can't change what happened 1 minute ago, yet alone a week or years ago. I hear so much of people who do this and it's so damaging. In order for YOU to actually be happy, in order for YOU to live a healthy and happy life which deep down, is what we all want, you have to LET GO of the past and more importantly, MAKE PEACE with it. If you don't you just won't move forward, I could come back to you in 5 or even 10 years from now and you'll be the same person doing the same things… how tragic is that, life is short enough as it is and far too short for us to be WASTING it sitting down and thinking about all the situations and experiences we can't change… yet people still do it, I haven't a clue what they think they're going to achieve, well they aren't thinking, that's the point. What I do instead is to put effort into every day. Each morning when I wake up, I give 110% effort, no matter what day it is or what I'm doing, even if I'm just staying in the house. That way of life has been me for the past 3 years, instead I now look back in a different way, I look back at how far I've come, I look back at how much I've achieved in the past week, month, or year. Why don't we do that instead, to look back at the past, but in a positive and healthy way. I don't care what situation you're in, you've got to stop looking back at the things you can't change… start tomorrow or start today, decide today that this is the day you're going to make a pact to yourself that you will put the effort in, you will try as hard as you possibly can, YOU will be the BEST version of yourself that you can possibly be... you'll do it with what you've got, no matter how little money or resources you have right now (which I know from experience can be so challenging), you're going to do whatever it takes to turn your life around, to achieve what you want to achieve. I could sit with you in a room for 5 hours straight talking about what you need to do, but then after that if you don't do anything in order to change it, then that may as well have been for nothing. It reminds me of that famous saying, *"you can take a horse to water, but you can't make it drink"*. The point is that no matter how much you want to change a past situation, you can't, but the exciting and euphoric thing is that YOU CAN CHANGE YOUR FUTURE, just writing this fills me with energy, you CAN make your future amazing. Dedicate to this every single day, no matter how slow the progress it's still progress, and if you're trying and actually caring to change or do something different with your life, that's all that matters. I don't care how small the results are either, because you're trying to achieve whatever it is you're working towards, it brings me back to the tortoise and the hare, don't always think that the people who are running at 100 miles an hour are achieving more than you, appearances can be very deceiving.

Chapter 37
Consistency is Key

At this point of reading I'm thinking you've now got a good idea of the aspects of your life you want to change, be this to set more goals for yourself, have a change in work, meet new people... it will be different for each person, or maybe you're not sure on how to move forward right now, which is also ok. The thing that's been the most important for me over the past 3 years has been consistency, this is key in order to have real lasting change, not something that lasts 2 minutes and then everything goes back to normal after that. For me I knew that I had to do my manifesting every day, my meditation and self-love, even when I'm away from home or on holiday you can absolute bet, I'll be spending time doing all my morning and evening routine. There has been various reports that having a solid morning and evening routine is the key to success, do you have either of these, but more importantly, is it a healthy one? One persons could be rolling out a of bed each morning feeling stressed before the day's even begun, then to glug coffee before rushing out the door... does something similar to this sound familiar? Having a routine like this will surely mean you're going to be feeling uptight and miserable before even starting your day. You're ALL worth so much more than that.

Some people might say they don't have time for a proper morning or evening routine, my answer to that, WAKE UP EARLIER, it will be more than worth your while I promise you. For me I try and wake up gradually, eat breakfast, do my practices, self-love and then once on my morning 30-minute commute on the train instead of scrolling through social media or reading a newspaper like most people I'll go to the notes section on my phone with my daily gratitude list and then my list of goals I want to achieve within the next year. I love my routine and I still remember life before I did any of that, definitely not as fun and the feeling this routine gives me is truly priceless… when I arrive in the city to start my day I arrive feeling refreshed and, in my ZONE, that's a word I say a lot… once I'm in my zone I'm ready for the day to come no matter what it throws at me. Am I saying that because I do this, I won't have any issues throughout my day, of course not, this is real life. Yes, sometimes things may happen, but the way I handle these situations is much calmer, much more grounded because I made the effort that morning to center myself and get in a positive mindset. I'm sure if everyone did this we wouldn't have as much road rage; we wouldn't have as many stressed out workers before they even reach their office.

So, I ask you for your next mission, to create a new morning routine. It doesn't have to be a huge radical change but doing small things I've suggested throughout this book will definitely make a difference to your day, even your weekend too. Evening routines for me will always be filled with a meditation after a busy day, it just gets me in that relaxed and most importantly BALANCED state, where everything through mind and body feels just so. Due to both positive or what we may think are negative factors will make us off balance, when I'm on a high and feeling excited about something I love to meditate then, the feeling of excitement is a great one but then having those short 20 minutes for myself just balances everything out… So many people think meditation is for stressed people… I'm not usually stressed, quite the opposite, it just makes me feel good and gives me more energy to smash my day.

Back to the point of the chapter, consistency. I could have easily decided after 6 months, a year, or less that I was fine without my practices now and to go back to normal, but you just can't do that. See it like this, imagine you go to the gym and then suddenly after 6 months of consistent exercise you decide to stop, do you think the current condition your body is in will stay that way now you've stopped going... of course NOT! So, when you stop being mindful will your headspace stay the same, I doubt it, it won't be long before the negative thoughts come creeping back in, and we all know how easily that can happen on a daily basis. So, my advice to you is to ALWAYS be consistent with the way you live your life, if you want to live a happy and healthy life and see the results you're creating you can't stop, don't see doing any of this as a chore either because then it definitely won't work, or at least to the same effect as it would if you're doing it because you genuinely want to.

So, how are you planning on improving your morning routine? Getting up and glugging a coffee and skipping breakfast is one I hear of quite a bit, it's certainly not a routine that's going to give you fire in your belly for a successful day, is it? I find that for me, waking up earlier so I'm not rushing around like a headless chicken works wonders, and that's before I've done any of my practices or looked over my gratitude list. Sometimes when it's a dark winter morning and I wake up it can be hard to feel as good as you do in the summer months, so then especially it's even more important to have a solid routine in place so you're ready to face the day with the best foot forward. So, how are you going to change your routine?

Chapter 38

We're More Similar than we Realise

  I spoke earlier about how we're all different, which is true, but something I've come to realise and realising more and more is that actually, we're all pretty similar, we just don't realise it because we're too busy wrapped up in our own lives and our own issues that we're facing. 1 in 4 of us will experience a mental health issue at least once in our lifetime, this could be anything from anxiety to depression to something like anorexia, and many more for that matter. Recently I filmed a mini documentary with a group of film students about confidence, and how this can be affected by mental health issues. I mentioned in the chapter about my own brush with mental health, getting badly bullied as a child certainly left its mark, and as a result it did affect my confidence, badly if I'm being honest. I feel so lucky that as I sit here today, I can say that's no longer the case, my confidence seems to be growing by the day, but it didn't happen overnight. During filming we spoke with people on the street about mental health, we spoke to many people, groups of teenagers, parents and their children and even a singer who had just finished performing. All of them had either suffered directly with a mental health issue or knew someone very close to them who had, it really opened my eyes to the fact that we're all pretty similar, yes we may be different and all have our own way of doing things but actually when it really comes down to it, we're all the SAME, we all want the same things, to be loved and feel LOVE, to be ACCEPTED and to be able to be our TRUE selves, that's all we really crave when you get down to the actual foundations of it all. Fancy cars and houses may be nice, but it's not what gives us that euphoric feeling of happiness, you may think it does but maybe you're trying to find happiness in a materialistic sense because you're not feeling acceptance, you're not feeling loved, maybe.

Another thing this experience taught me was that sometimes, particularly with mental health, you think you're the only one who's suffered something, or you're the only one who could be thinking like that, again, I've learnt that's definitely not the case. An example being when one of the participants we interviewed said that having the confidence they now have means they can do simple things and not have to worry, such as ordering food in a restaurant or ordering something at a bar. Something clicked in me when they said this and immediately bought me back to quite a different time. The thing is that I used to struggle with this, when they said it, I remember thinking to myself, *"oh my god, you're not the only one who used to find that difficult"*. Just because people don't usually say it out loud or talk about it doesn't mean they aren't suffering; it doesn't mean they aren't going through something too. Not anymore but this is something that used to be an issue. Thankfully, these days it's something I don't think twice about and probably never will again, ordering food is just a normal thing, but it certainly wasn't always. I don't care how silly that may sound, I'm being honest because I'm more increasingly aware of how many of us suffer but just don't talk about it, if it means I have to share these things which will help people relate and not feel alone, then so be it. No one deserves to feel alone or feel like they're the only one going through something.

This experience definitely taught me that there will always be someone out there who can relate to you, maybe from some of the things I've spoken about in this book you can relate to me too? So just remember, you might initially judge someone based on something they say, maybe they have different beliefs to you, but underneath all the physical stuff, we're all just human, we all want the same things in life, some just don't see it for a little while, it certainly took me a little while to realise what I actually needed in order to be happy. I used to think it lied in designer clothes, in how many social media followers or likes I had, boy was I in for a wakeup call.

Just Talk!

Talking about mental health isn't always an easy thing for some people, looking at people's body language and expressions during the interviews I could tell just how hard it was for them to express what they had been through, what clear pain they were experiencing by opening up the flood gates to talk about it. When I speak about mental health and my own experiences, I don't feel pain anymore, but for a long, long time I did, and couldn't even speak about it or if I'm honest, acknowledge to myself it was happening when it clearly was. I still have my moments though, and most likely, always will, but that's totally OK because I now have the tools to deal with it, it's like I have a mental toolbox crammed full of different things I can do to get back to my version of balanced, my version of calm. For me I'll go and meditate for a bit, go and speak with my Mom who always helps validate my thoughts and on countless occasions has made me realise I'm not going crazy, that it is ok, thank-you so much for that Mom.

I still have days when I'm not feeling so confident, when I'd rather throw on a hoodie or something comfortable and blend into the background... the one thing I've never really managed to do... oh well, I guess some people were just born to STAND OUT, and listen, you've gotta EMBRACE it, who cares if I'm a bit out there and extra, I love my personality and I think that's the thing I had to crack way back on my journey, acceptance. If you don't accept yourself as you are, the imperfectly amazing way you are then there's no way you can give love to others, there's no way you can be HAPPY. Acceptance will happen eventually, that I can promise, but like I said earlier, the time scale for each person is totally different. For me it happened fully when I was 18, just coming up to 19, I see fully confident teenagers at 16 in relationships and living their very best lives, that wasn't the case for me but again, there's NO RUSH and that is 100% ok, some of us are more slow burners than others. The people that may have been like that at 16 may face different issues later on in life or might not at all, that's just the way it can be depending on who you are, your past experiences, even genetic makeup, there's probably a million plus explanations as to why we're the way we are.

Chapter 39
Forgiveness sets us Free

You're now nearing the end now of exploring how you can become the very best YOU. It takes love, acceptance but also, forgiveness in order to bless the past and approach the future with a fresh mindset and a positive attitude.

In order to move on we have to forgive, I've left this till later on because although it may be the most important aspect, it's also hard, when I say hard, I mean damn hard and I'm talking from experience here. Forgiving someone, no matter what they've done is a hard process. I had to forgive my Dad for everything that happened growing up. For so many years I let this consume and affect me, to great lengths, I'm sure you can immediately think of someone you need to forgive? From not forgiving my Dad it affected me in different aspects of my own life, it really did. I had this moment where I knew in order for me to be happy and to have a new relationship with him, I had to forgive and say that yes, these things have happened, but finally we're moving on and won't speak of them again. That's another thing I think, there's forgiveness but then there's real forgiveness, when you choose to forgive someone but then don't fully let go of the pain they caused you and the things they did... this just isn't real forgiveness and won't give you that closure that you so desperately need. Real forgiveness is saying that you forgive that person and everything that happened, that a new fresh start will develop, it's the only way to truly be happy. Yes, I know it sounds incredibly cliché, but forgiveness sets you free.

I think when we forgive, I mean truly forgive like I did, we see new horizons and realise what's possible. It's going back to what I was saying earlier about moving forward, we have to let go, we have to accept that what has happened in the past has happened, and we can't do anything now to change it, but, we can make our future absolutely amazing, we truly can bless the past and forgive. Choosing to forgive is a big deal, it can almost feel like a weakness at times, choosing to forgive and be the bigger person, but trust me, the feeling you get from it is a good one and I urge you ALL to choose forgiveness, I know for different people this will be utterly hard and not something you'll want to do, but if you can find it within yourself to do so, then you'll be able to move on and live your best life even more than you ever could.

How about ourselves though? How many of us hold grudges with ourselves, for something we did or said, it might be 5 years ago, but we still beat ourselves up and basically hold ourselves prisoner, something I've been guilty of in the past. We seem to hold ourselves to higher standards, if others mess up, we tell them not to feel bad about it and not to worry. However, if we mess up, we badly judge ourselves and really beat ourselves up... why the hell don't we practice what we preach to others? It's like we have one set of rules for others and a totally different set for ourselves. We need to stop being so damn hard on ourselves, it gets us nowhere, we need to be our very own BEST FRIEND. Yes, this might sound cringey but it's the only way to true happiness. I'm my own best friend finally, in that way I've done a total 360. I went from beating myself up, talking negatively about myself to now genuinely loving the person I am and not beating myself up when I do things wrong... because I'm only HUMAN. If I can change the relationship I have with myself I know for absolute certain that anyone else can too.

So, forgive yourself. Yes, you may have upset someone, you may have annoyed a friend, you may have done something so bad that you feel utterly embarrassed, I could go on and on. NOBODY is perfect, I make mistakes constantly. I see mistakes as lessons, when we make a mistake it means we learn a lesson at the same time, in order to grow and live as a human being we have to make mistakes, we just have to. Yes, you might have offended someone on purpose, maybe you were in a negative space and you were lashing out for that reason, it's still CRUCIAL that now, in this very moment, you decide to LET IT GO and FORGIVE yourself, it's time to forgive, only then you can truly enjoy the now and move towards the future in a positive and refreshed state.

I think the problem a lot of the time is that we end up making things difficult for ourselves, not others, but mostly, us. We put ourselves down, we cause unnecessary drama, we judge ourselves, the list is endless. Some of this is down to society, some of it is down to our past and what we've experienced. Actually, a lot of our past influences how we view experiences today, how we view people and why we do the things we do. I used to let the past influence my daily life to the max I can honestly say. I'd let what happened in the past make me feel negative about positive experiences, I'd be instantly suspicious, question them and say they were too good to be true, a phrase I used a lot back then, its self-sabotage as its finest. The past was still affecting me, and this needed to change. I can safely say from experience, releasing the past is the hardest thing to do, it takes time, it takes resilience, it takes PATIENCE, but, its beyond worth it. Its saying that the past is the past, what's happened has happened and there's nothing I can do to change it, in order to live in the now and be happy, you have to release the past and no longer let it rule your life.

Those thoughts of the past will pop up quite a bit, I'm being honest here. Each time they come up you whack them back down like the whack a mole game I used to play as a child, and then you whack it down again, and again, and again. This will take TIME, but the longer you think positive thoughts, the less negative thoughts and negative thoughts about your past you'll experience... you'll need to trust me with this one. Ultimately, what I've learnt is that we need to get out of the way of OURSELVES, we are literally making things harder for ourselves, usually without even realising it. We need to stop the moaning, stop the complaining and take 100% RESPONSIBILITY for ourselves and our LIVES. Yes, we mess up, yes, we don't always get it right... nobody does. When we get out of our own way and see what we really need to do to be happy, it isn't hard, it's pretty simple, we're just not taught it growing up, we're not taught it in school, but actually, it's probably the most important thing we do need to know.

I've almost spoke about these different elements in the order they need to happen. 2 almost 3 years ago there is no way I could have forgiven my Dad for the past, I just couldn't, I wasn't in the headspace I'm in now. Back then the first thing I needed to do was to start loving myself, to then start accepting myself, to then start exploring my personality which lead to me doing different things and the different experiences I've spoken about within this book. Forgiveness won't happen first; we have to work towards that. I didn't have a time plan that by a certain time I'd forgive and be able to move on, I wish it was that simple, but this is life and it really isn't. There came a day when I just knew, I couldn't hold on to this anymore, it was making me physically ill, it was making me feel mentally ill, that's what grudges and holding bad feelings can do, they can manifest themselves as anxiety in your body, something I never knew until I experienced them for myself.

Without even realising it, I was making myself worse for years without even knowing it, I'd say that I had moved on but looking back now, it's clear to see that I hadn't moved on at all, I wasn't "over it", that's when I had the lightbulb moment, it literally felt like an epiphany, and I don't care how crazy or weird that might sound. I just knew there was something I had to do which would mean I'd be even happier and healthier, I was still in an amazing place but doing this has honestly meant I feel clearer than ever, for the first time I have real clarity and can see things for exactly what they are, which is a good thing because I'm in a better headspace, I feel better about the situations I've experienced and know they've shaped me. It takes a brave person to say that everything I've experienced in my life, particularly the major life events, I wouldn't change them, not one. They've SHAPED ME into the Jack I am now. If I hadn't had the majority of these life experiences I wouldn't be here now writing this book in the hope of making others feel good too, I know for sure I wouldn't. It's because of the adversity I've faced, it's because of the poor mental health I've had, it's because of the damaging experiences I've had that I'm WHERE I AM NOW, on the other side looking back, a safe distance away, just reflecting, just observing... it's a much better place to be than being in a tunnel of darkness wondering when you're going to find the light again.

I speak to countless individuals who speak to me and say they feel things won't get any better, and no, I can't give you a 100% promise that things will work out like a fairy tale, because this is life my friend and it rarely works out like the Hollywood movies do. However, what I can say is that there is always **HOPE**, there is always **LOVE** and there is always a **FUTURE**. If you're alive right now then there is a future for you, it can be whatever you want it to be, just because the previous chapters have all had the same themes and trends doesn't mean that the next one needs to. The next one can be **NEW**, the next one can be **UNIQUE** and **DIFFERENT**. Who cares if you're judged, who cares if you do something different and feel weird for a while, you have the power to decide that from now, changes will be occurring for you and your life. You don't need the change of a new year, I hate the bullshit of new year's resolutions, we all know that most of us will make them and give up by the time February arrives. I don't care if it's a Monday, Tuesday, Wednesday, Thursday, Friday, Saturday or Sunday as you're reading this now… tomorrow is a **NEW DAY** and **a NEW START** for whatever you want to happen. Give it baby steps, as you know by now that's what I did for a long while, it was baby steps, I didn't want to overwhelm myself, I made small but frequent changes over several years, which eventually, led to life changing results that you are now witnessing. I don't care how small the goal is or how insignificant you might think it is, everyone has to start **SOMEWHERE**, this isn't a **RACE**, this isn't a **COMPETITION**, it's your **JOURNEY** and nobody else's.

Chapter 40
Thank You!

My goodness, would you believe it, you're now at the end of exploring how you can become the very best version of yourself, how you can change your life in order to achieve your dreams and live your very BEST LIFE. Writing this has been a labor of love, I almost don't want to stop, it's been therapeutic putting everything down onto paper and getting to explain different aspects of my life experiences, then getting to share them with total strangers is quite a liberating feeling. I'm not perfect, I make mistakes, I don't have all the answers and I may not even be qualified, but, I know what works for me, I understand the power of our thoughts and how POSSIBLE it is to become the version of yourself that's already there, it honestly is, even if you don't realise it. When you've been a certain way for a long period of time it can become your normal, for me being in this mindset is my normal, but as you're all well aware now, it wasn't always and I've still lived longer in a poor mindset than I have in a healthy one, but I still wouldn't change it because if I hadn't have had these experiences, I wouldn't be fueled to spend 3 years of my life working on a book in the hopes of motivating and inspiring you. That's truly all I want to do, is to help, to offer advice and to learn myself along the way too, I'm only 21 and well aware I have a LOT of things to learn and life to discover.

I'm proud of you, immensely, especially if you're reading this now because it means you've stuck with it, even if you didn't agree with everything I said or suggested, you've seen it through, and I thank you for that. Every single one of you reading this is **BEAUTIFUL**, **STRONG** and most importantly, **RESILIENT**. You might be shaking your head to disagree, but I know that although you might have made mistakes, although you might have lashed out from a place of hurt and disappointment with your own life, the real YOU is there, it's there I promise you it's there. I think of it like fog, sometimes when you're feeling so low and in such a bad place all you can see is fog, you can't make sense of anything, nothing is going in your favor and you wonder why everyone else is having the luck and good times whilst you're watching on, again, like being in the passenger seat whilst the car is somehow driving itself. But you need to look deeper, much deeper, because amongst the fog somewhere there is a glimmer of **LIGHT**, a glimmer of **HOPE**, of **HAPPINESS**, of **COMFORT**. It might not seem like it, but it's there, it always was and always will be there, never forget that, no matter how dark times might get or how bumpy the track underneath becomes, the light is always there.

The biggest takeaway I can give you at this point in my life is to not worry so much, it takes up so much of our time we don't even realise. Stop worrying about the things that may never come, stop worrying about the past, that page has turned now and there's no going back. Stop worrying about the future so much too, we can't possibly predict what it will bring with complete accuracy, so please, **STOP TRYING**. Instead, lets enjoy the very **MOMENT** we're now in, let's be fearless, let's dance in the rain and just from time to time, **STOP CARING**, stop caring about the things that don't matter, let's stop thinking about what's out of our control, we can't be everywhere at once, we can't have the answers to every question, so let's stop trying.

We also need to SURRENDER too, we need to surrender to the things we can't control or even change, because not everything in life can always be changed, sometimes it's not meant to be. I always view surrendering like being in the sea, the sea of life almost. In the sea when we have hardships and troubles it's like the waves that will appear, usually without any warning or prediction. When these waves appear, we will try everything we can to FIGHT them, to fight the wave, but from doing this we will lose so much energy, we will try and try but it will easily overpower us before long, a recipe for total disaster. I used to fight waves daily, I'd feel exhausted, utterly tired with no energy from fighting the feelings I was experiencing. Instead, we need to SURRENDER. When we see the wave approaching instead of getting ready to fight it we need to instead LET IT BE, we need to let it wash over us and just surrender to the situation or feeling, but you might then think that from doing this you'll drown, but no, you WILL FLOAT, your body will float back to the surface, only then you'll realise how much better you feel from not getting caught up in the wave, from not getting caught up in the emotion and feeling of it all, surrendering is the key.

If you're not being true to yourself, if you're not living your truth and letting the world see the REAL YOU, you will never be fulfilled, you must know that, I need this to be the one thing you take away from this book. I was a fake me for such a long time that I know of the consequences, it can be anything from poor mental health to limiting beliefs to slow progress, all from wearing a mask, all from being too scared to show the world who I was. Now, I have to be myself because when I sat back and thought about it, it's actually the EASIEST thing any one of us will ever do, to just be ourselves. I thought doing it would be hard, it isn't, of course, it's the most natural thing in existence, to just be the **PERFECTLY IMPERFECT, AMAZING, BEAUTIFUL, POWERFUL YOU!** It was being the fake one that made me tired, that made me sad. I thought I had to change my clothes, my style, my voice or my interests in order to be a better me, but no, because everything I needed was **IN ME**. Everything I craved to be happy and to feel good about myself was all **INTERNALLY**, but all the while I was chasing the **EXTERNAL**, in people, in material objects, whilst the whole time I possessed it all inside and I had no idea at all. It's a big and hard fact to realise, in seeing that right now as you're reading this, everything you ever needed, everything you ever wanted, **IS ALL WITHIN YOU**, it's inside right now, it doesn't matter what you've done in the past, it doesn't matter the thoughts that are consuming you right now, in order to change all you need to do is look inside of YOURSELF for the answers, because trust me, you'll find them eventually, it's just about finding the right key to unlock the door… because when you do, when you do unlock it you'll know, it really is like living your life on a **WHOLE NEW LEVEL**. Remember too as you finish this reading, life isn't a fairy tale, it isn't a Hollywood movie, you'll **HAVE SETBACKS**, you'll **HAVE KNOCKBACKS**, you'll **HAVE CHALLENGES**… but, this is LIFE and that's totally OK… if you never experienced any of this I'd really wonder why, we all have troubles and issues every now and then, as you now hopefully understand, its more about how we **DEAL** and **RESPOND** to these challenges that makes all the difference, not the challenge itself, don't focus on that too much, focus on what you **DO NOW.**

So, reader, what happens next, what do you do now? You might want to change 101 things about yourself after reading this, but tackling one thing at a time is what will work the best, wanting to change everything will result in you feeling overwhelmed, and as you'll now see from my own journey, nothing changed overnight, it's been progress building and building, it's a journey of **GROWTH**, a journey of **CHANGE** and a journey of **LEARNING**... I still learn things daily about Jack that I never realised, just when I think I'm at a point of knowing everything something happens to make me realise that actually, I don't really have a clue and learn so much more than I ever did before. So don't beat yourself up, I don't care how old you are, **NOBODY IS A LOST CAUSE**, I say this statement so much because I'm constantly seeing people being labelled as lost causes, like they can't be helped, or they can't change... I will always be that person to stand up for them, because I know what I know and truly believe that every single human can become the version they want, be that a low or high version, its entirely up to **YOU**, not to society, not to your partner, your family, work colleagues or friends... but **YOU**, it's **YOU** who has the power to shape your future, it's **YOU** who has the power to change something, to do something different, to travel to a new place, and it's **YOU** who has the power to think new thoughts and to create a new routine, whatever it is, it's all down to **YOU**.

Now, I've got a world to go and motivate, will you join me?

I send you **LOVE, HAPPINESS & LIGHT**!

Thank you xo

About the Author

Jack Walton is a 21-year-old student from Birmingham in the UK. For the last 3 years he's worked on totally transforming his life in every way using the power of his mind, positive thinking and discovering the Law of Attraction. Along with this book Jack speaks about similar topics on his own social media profiles, follow @iamjackwalton for his personal profile and @motivatorboy for his business page. Content includes motivational videos and a monthly podcast Jack produces, 'A Slice of Life', which is available via iTunes and Spotify.

Along with this he is also a mental health advocate and has previously appeared on TV and in campaigns talking about the topic and continues to do so. Jack's mission is simple, to spread his message daily and to motivate people, whoever they may be, to become their very best self... to become the very best YOU!

Printed in Great Britain
by Amazon